PRAYING THE PSALMS

Learning to Pray with God's Words

Lawrence P. Duffield

TABLE OF CONTENTS

PRAY WITH GOD'S WORDS

"Prayer is finding a way to God and speaking with Him, whether the heart is full or empty." – Martin Luther

FOR MANY YEARS I HAD TROUBLE PRAYING, AND EVEN more trouble listening for God's answers. Listening to God through his Word in the Psalms has deepened my spiritual life more than anything else I've found. This book attempts to give forward what my teachers, pastors and fellow believers gave me.

God gave us the Psalms nearly 3000 years ago. What I learned recently is something that Christians have known, and taught each other, since the very beginning. Jesus showed his disciples who he was and why he came here by using this very same tool kit. The Book of Psalms, in the center of the Holy Scriptures, is a resource that nearly every Christian has in their house at this minute.

We don't teach each other how to pray. I suppose we assume the Holy Spirit will carry that load. However, if you give the prayer technique I'm going to lay out a serious try, many of you will transform your whole prayer life.

This book is not primarily about analyzing the Book of Psalms. There are whole libraries that do that. It is about a better way to pray, using the psalms as a guide. In these six sessions you can integrate the Book of Psalms into your prayer life in the way that Christians have done for nearly 2000 years. You will learn how to extract God's Word for you out of God's Words to all his people. Along the way, we look at how three important Christian writers, Martin Luther, C. S. Lewis and Dietrich Bonhoeffer, and a few other Christian disciples, used psalms in their own devotions, and examine how valuable a part of their spiritual life this Book was.

As interesting as the stories of these Christian lives are, though, their comments only form a counterpoint to your own prayer practice. The major outcome of this study will be a new skill set you can use for your personal prayers. This course is divided into six sessions, each designed to take about a week. In every session we integrate five new psalms into your prayer life and show you one way the Holy Spirit carries God's Word to you.

This prayer practice will probably add about 10 minutes a day to your prayer time, so allow for that extra bit of time to talk with God. Over the course of these sessions, you will develop a conversation with the scriptures. The Word of God for everyone embedded in the psalms will gradually become God's personal Word for you.

Beginning with the second session, we use the psalms that you prayed during the prior week to illustrate how psalms spoke to Jesus, Israel, the Church or one of the other Christians whose story we tell. Reflecting this way gives the Holy Spirit the chance to move your heart, while also looking at how that same Scripture affected someone else, perhaps in a very different way.

Praying from the heart

Modern Christians are heavily influenced by the idea that "authentic prayer" should come from our own feelings and thoughts. This idea comes from the late 18th Century Romantic notion that "natural" impulses are to be preferred over learned manners. There is something to be said for this. Prayer without thinking about what is being said is worship, but it isn't "talking with God". So far so good.

Left to ourselves, though, "natural" prayers are mostly "beginner's prayers". "God give me this"; "God make that happen"; "God, Help!" Unskilled prayers generally ask for "Yes" or "No" answers or tell God what we want him to do. God has far more to say to us than that! What if your child only talked to you when she couldn't think of any other alternative or if she wanted you to give her something? What parent wouldn't want more?

Cries of need or of anguish are valid prayers. God wants us to turn to him for all our needs. Still, there are better ways to talk to God and other times than in emergencies. Prayers help shape us into better Christians. To get the most from conversation with God, we need to learn how to listen to the other things he wants us to hear, besides "Yes" or "No". Without practice, we can't hear him, and our prayers become a wail of fear — "Where are you, God? I can't feel you!"

Another "beginner mistake" happens when we try to hide things from God. Genesis 3: 8–13 is the first record of human speech with God. What do you suppose that prayer was like? Adam and Eve were trying to hide from God that they'd eaten the fruit of the forbidden tree! Our first impulse, as the scripture writers knew, is to try to keep our faults out of the conversation. As if God doesn't know every one.

In the Book of Psalms, prayer is very different. As we'll see, the speaker is sometimes angry, or bewildered. Many psalms are about hurt, and their cries for help are wrenching. But the speaker knows God always listens, and answers, and the speaker, the psalmist hears that answer. God answers our prayers, too. We need to learn how to listen.

Psalms show both ends of the eternal conversation with God. Our cries – God's answers. Answers embedded into the Holy Scripture, given to us as an inheritance, as God's adopted children.

Prayers in the Bible

When you think about it, it seems odd that the Bible, which we call God's Word, has prayers from people to God. How can the people's prayers be God's Word?

The answer is pretty simple. We live in a fallen world, not the one we were created for. We can't, by ourselves, love God and come to him. But God takes care of that. The Holy Spirit inspires us and encourages us to trust him. Our faith is a gift from God. Prayers that come out of that faith are also gifts.

Conversation with God forms an eternal circle: God encourages us to speak to him by his gift of the Holy Spirit. By God's Grace we come to believe and trust. Then God answers our prayers, so that we learn to believe that he hears and wants this conversation. God's inspiring Word becomes our word to him, then he answers with his Word to us, and things happen. When we make the words of a psalm part of our prayer, they become our word to God. When those words come back to us with reassurance and trust, they are God's Word to us. This reciprocal experience is waiting to happen to every believer in every prayer.

God's Word created the whole world. John says in his gospel "through (Jesus, the Word) all things were made; without him nothing was made that has been made." (John 1:3). In a mystery we believe but cannot easily explain, the eternal Word that was with God, and was God, became flesh in Jesus Christ. Christ, the living Word, inspires and leads us to God through his example and his strength. This Word of God does more than speak to us. When God speaks, things happen. So it is completely understandable that we want to talk with God and have things happen to us.

The Holy Scriptures are a collection of written stories, poems, songs, histories and letters that God's people began assembling before Christ was born. Every "Book" tells part of our story, from when God created the world, to when the world was broken and twisted by sin, to God's choice of Abraham and Sarah bless the nations, to Moses, David and the prophets who foretold a Savior for all people. Then, in the New Testament, we hear of Jesus, God's Word made flesh, the Resurrection, and the story of the earliest Christians.

These stories, poems, songs, histories and letters describe a series of encounters between individuals and groups of people and the Living God. The Scriptures show, time and again, in story after story, what it looks like when God reveals himself to us. The Bible tells the whole story – the Scriptures hold nothing back. The Scriptures also bring God to us in many ways. Occasionally we hear God speak directly. We hear Moses and the Prophets talk to God and report his answers.

We see God act, revealing in unexpected ways who he is and how much he loves us. We watch God's people respond, see their triumphs and their errors. In the Book of Psalms, we see them talking to and about God, relating what he has done in their lives and what they hope he will do in the future.

Prayers in the Bible are different from most prayers. They're all over the map. God's people pray honestly, fearlessly. Sometimes they pray naively. They pray with joy, with rage, with despair or with doubt. The Bible's prayers are a living, passionate conversation with God.

In the Bible, the believer speaks – and God answers. For over three thousand years, the people of God, in the Scriptures, testify that this Scripture story is the truth – the real thing.

Psalms aren't the only prayers in the Bible. Scattered throughout the Scriptures are other prayers. We have already encountered Adam and Eve's conversation with God. In Genesis 18: 17–32 we see Abraham arguing, bargaining and pleading with God to spare Sodom and Gomorrah. It is high comedy to listen to Abraham trying to bargain God down to save whoever might be righteous in those cities. "If there aren't 50 righteous people, will you settle for 10?" God, who knows exactly how many righteous people there weren't in those two cities, goes right along as far as Abraham's courage will take him. How God must have been amused, and delighted, by the whole prayer. Already Abraham begins to care for everyone, righteous or not, just like God!

Look at Exodus 3:1 through 4:17. God tells Moses that he really is qualified to lead God's people to freedom. Moses, on the other hand, has a long list of reasons why he's just not the one and why God should pick somebody, anybody, else. Arguing with God is also prayer. Still, Moses listens as God shows him how to deal with every objection. That's a lesson for us, too. God will answer, and make things possible. We can hear God's answers when we learn to listen.

Now look at Exodus 15: 19–21. This is Miriam's Song, the Bible's first hymn. It is a song of celebration as the Hebrew fugitives are saved from Pharaoh's army at the Red Sea. Miriam's hymn of joy became one of the best loved songs of the Children of Israel. God's people knew to pray when they were bubbling over with happiness.

Ave Maria, gratia plena: Dominus tecum.

Ecce ancilla Domini: Fiat mihi secundum verbum tuum.

The New Testament – Mary's Prayer

More than 1000 years later, Jesus' mother, Mary, takes up Miriam's theme when she announces to her cousin Elizabeth what God has told her about her unborn child (Luke 1:46–55). We call Mary's song "The Magnificat" and it is one of the finest prayers in the whole Bible.

Listening to the Magnificat we get a clear idea why God might have chosen this particular teenager to be Jesus' mother. This wonderful prayer was voiced by a young girl from an out of the way village deep in the country. Mary shows her firm trust in God and her mastery of a rich heritage of personal prayer. Mary learned how to pray and trust God from the Holy Scriptures. We can, too.

Jesus Teaches Us to Pray

"Lord teach us to pray," the disciples begged. The "Lord's Prayer" is an excellent place to start when you want to learn to talk to God.

Jesus' prayer's greatest power is its completeness. Jesus brings a broad range of topics, attitudes and concerns to his Father. We can draw consolation, strength and hope from praying along with Jesus' prayer.

The greatest value of the Lord's Prayer to us does not come from exact repetition of the words. Instead, use it as a pattern into which you pour your personal concerns. When we fold a Bible prayer into our own prayers in this manner, we look closely at every line to see how it applies to our needs. When we do this, surprisingly often what we read in the Bible speaks directly to our day to day life. Carefully looking at each phrase in a bible passage is called a "close reading".

Martin Luther's Small Catechism shows how close reading works. "The Small Catechism" was designed to teach ordinary believers the basics of the Christian faith. Besides the Lord's Prayer, there are close readings for the Ten Commandments and the Apostle's Creed, and explanations of Holy Communion and Baptism. Luther felt that talking to God is the most reliable way to open our hearts to God's Word, and that thinking about God's Word and Sacraments while praying is the best way to talk to God. Take a closer look at how he does it. Here is Luther's "close reading" of the Lord's Prayer:

Explanation of the Lord's Prayer from Luther's Small Catechism

Our Father in heaven.

What does this mean?

God's name is certainly holy in itself, but we pray in this petition that it may be kept holy among us also.

How is God's name kept holy? God's name is kept holy when the Word of God is taught in its truth and purity, and we, as the children of God, also lead holy lives according to it. Help us to do this, dear Father in heaven! But anyone who teaches or lives contrary to God's Word profanes the name of God among us. Protect us from this, heavenly Father!

Your Kingdom Come.

What does this mean?

The kingdom of God certainly comes by itself without our prayer, but we pray in this petition that it may come to us also.

How does God's Kingdom come? God's kingdom comes when our heavenly Father gives us His Holy Spirit, so that by His grace we believe His holy Word and lead godly lives here in time and there in eternity.

Your will be done on earth as in heaven.

What does this mean?

The good and gracious will of God is done even without our prayer, but we pray in this petition that it may be done among us also.

How is God's will done? God's will is done when he breaks and hinders every evil plan and purpose of the devil, the world and our sinful nature, which do not want us to hallow God's name or let his kingdom come; and when He strengthens and keeps us firm in His Word and faith until we die. This is His good and gracious will.

Give us today our daily bread.

What does this mean?

God certainly gives daily bread to everyone without our prayers, even to all evil people, but we pray in this petition that God would lead us to realize this and to receive our daily bread with thanksgiving.

What is meant by daily bread? Daily bread includes everything that has to do with the support and needs of the body, such as food, drink, clothing, shoes, house, home, land, animals, money, goods, a devout husband or wife, devout children, devout workers, devout and faithful rulers, good government, good weather, peace, health, self-control, good reputation, good friends, and the like.

Forgive us our sins as we forgive those who sin against us.

What does this mean?

We pray in this petition that our Father in heaven would not look at our sins, or deny our prayer because of them. We are neither worthy of the things for which we pray, nor have we deserved them, but we ask that He would give them all to us by grace, for we daily sin much and surely deserve nothing but punishment. So we too will sincerely forgive and gladly do good to those who sin against us.

Lead us not into temptation.

What does this mean?

God tempts no one. We pray in this petition that God would guard and keep us so that the devil, the world, and our sinful nature may not deceive us or mislead us into false belief, despair, and other great shame and vice. Although we are attacked by these things, we pray that we may finally overcome them and win the victory.

But deliver us from evil.

What does this mean?

We pray in this petition, in summary, that our Father in heaven would rescue us from every evil of body and soul, possessions and reputation, and finally, when our last hour comes, give us a blessed end, and graciously take us from this valley of sorrows to Himself in heaven.

For the kingdom, the power, and the glory are Yours, now and forever. Amen.

What does this mean?

This means that I should be certain that these petitions are pleasing to our Father in heaven, and are heard by Him; for He Himself has commanded us to pray in this way and has promised to hear us. Amen means "yes, yes, it shall be so."

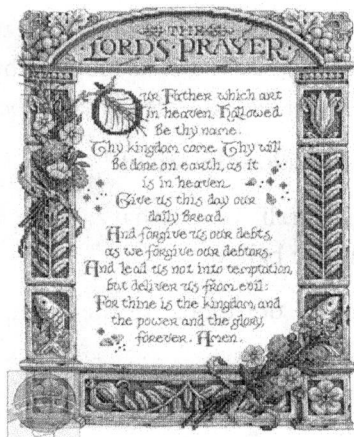

THE LORD'S PRAYER

Our Father which art in heaven, Hallowed be thy name. Thy kingdom come. Thy will be done on earth, as it is in heaven. Give us this day our daily bread. And forgive us our debts, as we forgive our debtors. And lead us not into temptation, but deliver us from evil: For thine is the kingdom, and the power and the glory, forever. Amen.

Luther praying at Philip Melanchton's bedside

Prayer using a Close Reading

Try out a close reading. Read the Lord's Prayer one petition at a time. Then read Luther's explanation, and focus your prayer on really talking to God alongside Jesus the way Luther does. Let God's Son be your prayer teacher and let the Holy Spirit guide your thoughts.

Other parts of the Bible record several of Jesus' teachings about prayer. For example, Luke 18: 1 — 16 is a collection of three of Jesus' sayings. As you would expect, the advice is excellent, the focus tight:

"Ask for what you want. Don't be afraid."

"Don't use prayer to tell God what a fine fellow you are or how lucky He is that you believe in Him."

"Trust like a little child – don't look for the catch."

How well Jesus knows his people!

Why Psalms?

This study uses Psalms as a frame for personal prayer. We will look closely at many psalms, paying attention to what the writer is saying, and what questions he asks God. This will not be an academic exercise: we will be incorporating whatever we hear in the psalms into our personal conversations with God.

Psalms don't replace our everyday prayers. Rather we add the Word of God found in the Psalms to the rest of our prayer. The goal is to focus on topics and worries that we wouldn't ordinarily consider, and to listen while God answers our prayers.

During such a composite prayer, think about each phrase. Give yourself scope to be creative. You will make connections between everyday life and your prayer life that you might otherwise overlook. The Book of Psalms is packed with layer on layer of meaning, some of which speaks to you today, through words and phrases which are thousands of years old.

If "close reading" is something you have done before, you already know the value of widening God's conversation with you. If this is new, you are beginning a real adventure – a somewhat scary one. Don't worry, you are in the very best of hands – God's. Close reading takes practice, but it will soon become a natural part of your prayer.

Psalms were part of the Hebrew Bible well before Jesus's day. Psalms feel contemporary, even though they were collected 2200 years ago. That's because God already knows our every concern, and the Holy Spirit is always prepared to guide us through life's challenges.

Prayers, promises and themes from Psalms saturate the Gospels. Psalms and Isaiah are the Books most quoted by Jesus. He uses them to show his disciples – and the skeptics around him – who he is and what his ministry is all about.

Early Christians used Psalms extensively for prayers and songs, for the same reason Jesus used them – they describe and identify who exactly the Messiah, the Christ, is.

Today Christians use Psalms for praise and thanksgiving and to help understand Jesus' place in God's plan for the world. Psalms has more descriptions of God than anywhere else in the Bible. Psalms is all about God, about our troubles, and about how we fit into God's creation.

The Book of Psalms is a part of the Jewish and Christian canon. Each psalm, we testify, is a true conversation with and from God. Psalms are a believer's words to God. They are also God's Word to us. What better place can we go for instruction in how to pray?

We listened to Luther's close reading of the Lord's Prayer. Now try it for yourself on the Twenty-third Psalm. The 23rd Psalm is the most loved of all the psalms. Christians sing, chant or recite it in worship. You may have memorized it for Catechism or Sunday School.

Our goal is to listen carefully to what the psalm says, and hear your thoughts in response. There are no "right answers". Each reading of a psalm carries its meaning to the person praying. There are lots of correct meanings, including the one where God talks directly to you.

The Good Shepherd – graffiti in the Roman Catacombs

This is your "solo flight". You might write a one or two sentence "What does this mean?" answer of your own as you work through this psalm.

The text below is from the King James translation of the Bible (sometimes called the Authorized Version). The 23rd Psalm in the KJV is one of the finest pieces of English poetry ever written. It recreates the mood and the awe that David felt while thinking about how deep was God's regard for him and how richly he had been blessed.

I have included pertinent observations from other readers, below, to give an idea of what sort of thoughts may turn up in your prayer.

Here we go.

The 23rd Psalm

1. "The Lord is my shepherd; I shall not want."

What does this mean?

David's opening is deeply layered. Of all the "gods", YHWH and no other is my shepherd. The Lord God cares for me as a shepherd cares for his flock; The Lord is my king and ruler. The Lord will provide whatever I need - though not necessarily everything I want.

2. "He maketh me to lie down in green pastures: he leadeth me beside the still waters,"

What does this mean?

The land of Canaan is a desert and savannah. The lush meadow pictured here is a shepherd's vision of paradise.

3. he restoreth my soul. He leadeth me in the paths of righteousness for his name's sake.

What does this mean?

David turns to God for his peace of mind, and God shows him how to lead a God-filled life. It pleases God to do this. God is delighted to show the world what following God looks like.

4. Yea, though I walk through the valley of the shadow of death, I will fear no evil: for thou art with me; thy rod and thy staff, they comfort me.

What does this mean?

David's Lord protects and keeps him within the bounds of safety. Whatever dangers and trouble await, God will be there beside him.

5. Thou preparest a table before me in the presence of mine enemies; thou anointest my head with oil; my cup runneth over.

What does this mean?

David's enemies are still around, but God visibly blesses David and shows him favor. More favor than he can contain.

6. Surely goodness and mercy shall follow me all the days of my life; and I will dwell in the house of the Lord forever.

What does this mean?

David turns from remembering past blessings to confident trust and hope for future blessing. This sequence is typical of the way the psalms open us to recognize and acknowledge God's love.

Thinking About It:

- Are David's prayers similar to your own?

- How is this psalm different from your usual prayers?

- What do you think makes this psalm pleasing to God?

- Christians invariably picture Christ as the "Good Shepherd" in Psalm 23. Do you think this is an appropriate application of David's imagery?

What does this mean? – Listening to God's Word for You

The 23rd Psalm is around 3000 years old. It was likely composed by King David, probably early in his career. It has been a favorite of Israelite, Jewish and Christian worship. David's Psalm comes to us as God's Word, in the Hebrew Scriptures and in the Christian "Old Testament" alike.

Psalm 23 is a prayer to God. It is also God's Word to us. Here is a brief look at how God's people heard this Word down through the centuries.

David's Thanksgiving

In the 23rd Psalm David, called to be Shepherd King of Israel, rejoices at God's blessing, at how God protects, exalts and justifies him. He is confident that he "will dwell in the House of the Lord forever". The 23rd psalm bubbles over with David's awed thanks. You can hear the amazement and happiness in his voice. This is a very personal prayer from a young man still overjoyed at the abundance of God's gifts.

Israel's Joy

David's psalm was used in Israel's worship, song and festival. Through good and bad times in his life and those of the later kings, this psalm was testimony to Israel's faith that the Lord would protect them and that Abraham's descendants would prosper like David. The Words did not change – Israel heard a very different message – one addressed to Abraham's descendants.

By the Rivers of Babylon

Through sin, Israel's faith in God's love turned into a conviction that God would never let anything happen to "His People" no matter how badly they treated the poor, widow or stranger, or how many of Moses' Ten Commandments went by the wayside. They ignored prophetic warnings, and persecuted God's messengers. Eventually, the United Kingdom, Israel and Judah, quarreled, split, then were conquered one by one by the emerging empires of Assyria and Babylon. At last the remnant of Judah's elite was carried off to Babylon, eating "the bitter bread of Exile", a phrase that comes down to us from this time.

The 23rd Psalm formed part of a frayed thread by which the faithful held on to their belief that God would somehow forgive, rescue them, and redeem his promise to David. David's psalm of thanks became the Remnant's lifeline. Once again, the Words were the same – what was different was God's message.

Rededication and Rebuilding

At last the Exile ended, and the descendants of the Exiles returned to Judea. They cleared away the debris and began work on another Temple in thanks to the God who brought them home. The Psalms, including the 23rd, were messages of determination. God had not forsaken Israel, now Israel would dedicate themselves to God, as had David. With God the shepherd, how could things go wrong? The Word did not change – but the message shifted once again.

I will Fear no Evil

The people of Israel never did regain the glorious Kingdom that God gave to David's care. They rebuilt the Temple, but ignored God's call for righteousness. God's warning, given by the prophets so long ago, was also passed over: "Do you think that, if I desired the flesh of animals, I would turn to you? The hillsides are covered with my flocks." Judah twisted and turned but could not escape the results of its apostasy.

Empires of the Ancient World washed over Judea again and again. Alexander the Great and his Successors conquered Palestine. The Maccabees rebelled, briefly triumphed, then quarreled and fell.

The Roman Empire engulfed Israel. Judea was a client Kingdom, all policy was set by Rome. Roman legions enforced a Roman peace. Zealots plotted revolution. Scribes and pharisees longed for the Messiah, the Davidic King, who would set them free. Mystics withdrew into the desert to wait for the apocalypse. Common people prayed the psalms and waited.

In this unsettled world, the 23rd Psalm became a word portrait of the long awaited Savior who would set the world right again. The same words, but a new Word of hope for God's people to cling to.

God's Son

Jesus, the Messiah from Nazareth, turned Israel's understanding of the Davidic Messiah topsy turvy. Walking humbly, his birth in the city of David was heralded to shepherds and the poor, but went unremarked by Israel's powerful or learned. At the climax of his ministry, he entered Jerusalem on a donkey, not in a chariot, heralded with palm fronds, not spears. Jesus confounded expectations – this was not the Word they were listening for. Not Triumphant Liberator but Suffering Servant. His crucifixion and death at the hands of his enemies was the last way Israel expected God to fulfill his promise. Then, on the third day, Jesus rose from the tomb. God's promise can't be killed.

God's blessing to David recorded in places like the 23rd Psalm formed a clear template. Christians recognized their unexpected Savior from the Scriptures: Jeremiah, Isaiah, Psalms. Everyone knew the words – but God's Word surprised them all.

The Good Shepherd Today

The 23rd Psalm paints a vivid picture of our Shepherd King. Jesus' life and resurrection is an assurance that we also have a Good Shepherd to lead us and bless our life. As David foresaw, we will "dwell in the House of the Lord, forever." God's blessings for David, his promise to Israel and Christ's promise to the whole world come to us in the exact same words, carrying layer on layer of old and new meanings: to David, to Israel, to Christendom. To you and me.

> "So shall my word be that goeth forth out of my mouth: it shall not return unto me void, but it shall accomplish that which I please, and it shall prosper in the thing whereto I sent it." [Isaiah 55:11 KJV]

Explore a new, and very old, way to pray. In the Book of Psalms, the Holy Spirit helps us listen as God answers our prayers.

Practical Exercise:

Review your prayer practices

With all this in mind, let's build a base line of experience. Ask yourself these questions. Make a brief note of your answers so that you can look at them as if they were from a friend or family member.

Occasional Prayer

Do you often pray outside of formal worship?

Intercessory Prayer

Do you pray specifically for people you know?

Daily Prayer

Do you typically pray at the start or at the end of the day? At meals?

Do you use printed devotional materials or mediations?

Do you have family prayer?

This is where you're starting. Put the note aside for a few weeks so you can see the change in your prayer life.

This Week in Prayer

Use psalms this week in your daily prayer. Each prayer will take about 10 minutes more than usual. Be as honest to God as you know how. Don't forget to listen: these psalms are also God's Word to you.

There are five psalms below. Compare your other prayers with "prayer plus psalm" to get a sense of how psalms mesh with your prayer life.

The Holy Spirit has been at work in our lives for decades – there is a lot of interesting spiritual material in your life for God to work with. Give yourself a chance to hear what God has to say.

The psalms below are samples of the main types of psalm. Praying them provides you a background for the discussion in the next chapter, when we talk about how the Book of Psalms is put together and see how Hebrew poetry works when translated into nearly every language.

It is important that you encounter psalms for yourself in prayer before you read "about" them. As an academic study, the Book of Psalms is fascinating. As a way to open the Scriptures to believers, praying the psalms is life changing. Everything we will say in this study is aimed to help you better hear God's Word in prayer.

Prayer Psalms:

Psalm 1 – "Blessed is the man ...."

Psalm 4 – "Answer me when I call to you, O my righteous God."

Psalm 13 – "How long, O Lord? Will you forget me forever?"

Psalm 104 – "Praise the Lord, O my soul."

Psalm 126 – "When the Lord brought back the captives to Zion"

Thinking About It

- Is praying with a psalm easier? Harder? Different?

- Were some psalms easier to pray than others? Why?

- Did praying with psalms suggest new things to pray about?

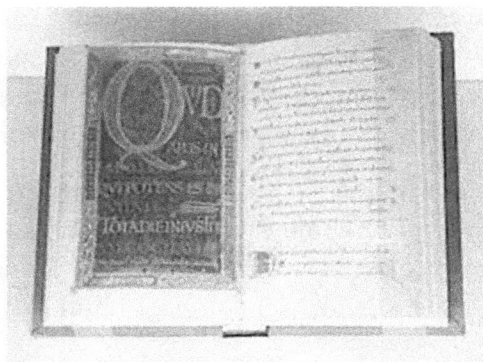

The Dagulf Psalter - 8th Century, made for Hildegaard, Charlemagne's Queen

INTRODUCTION TO PSALMS

IN BIBLE STUDY, AN "INTRODUCTION" IS NOT A CLASS for beginners. "Introductions" sum up what we know or guess about how a part of the Bible was collected, how it was passed along to us and what it was used for, who were the original hearers, the meaning of particular unusual or important phrases, words or expressions, and how God's people have found it to be particularly useful over the years.

Take the word "Shepherd" in the Bible. In some psalms that might literally refer to one who tends sheep. Alongside the literal meaning, the phrase may also indicate that the psalmist is speaking of Israel's King. Or it might be read as an image of God, who leads Israel's King "in the paths of righteousness" like a good shepherd leads his flock. "Introductions" point these things out as they occur.

To a believer who simply wants to listen to God's Word and pray, these details may seem of lesser importance. Still, familiarity with the Book of Psalms, as a document, is useful to understand why Psalms is such an important part of Christian (and Jewish) spiritual life. This material can also point to some of the hidden layers of meaning contained in every psalm, ready to convey God's Word to the reader.

This chapter is the academic part of our study. For reasons of space and focus, we'll keep it short. If you are just beginning to read the Bible you can skip forward and come back when you have more experience praying with psalms and want to go deeper. Still, this material will open your eyes to just how much meaning can be packed into one short book.

A side note: academic study of the Bible relies in part on informed guesses and observations based on small clues. We try very hard here to separate things we know from things we only think might be true.

The main evidence we have for what is in the Bible is in the Bible itself. God's Holy History predates academic history by a couple of thousand years. We don't have anyone but God to ask the questions that come

Psalter arranged for choral singing

to mind when we read the Bible. Instead of documents, we rely on generations of believers who testify that this is God's Word and on their assurance that it contains all we need to know about the story.

Authorship and Transmission

Psalms is the most important book in the third part of the Holy Scripture, the "Writings".

The Writings include Proverbs, Job, Song of Songs, Ruth, Lamentations, Ecclesiastes, Esther, Daniel, Ezra-Nehemia and I & II Chronicles. Like them, Psalms is "Wisdom" literature, and its final editors were concerned with practical issues like obedience to God's Law, faithfulness and right conduct.

This material was first assembled in David's day and assembly continued until sometime after the Babylonian exile. About 200 BC, at the latest, editors polished, arranged and prepared this material into the Book of Psalms we have today. At about the same time, scholars translated Psalms into Greek for the benefit of a growing number of Jews who were scattered around the Mediterranean basin and no longer spoke Hebrew.

Many of the psalms were composed much earlier in Israel's history. King David wrote some, though we're not certain which ones. David definitely wrote psalms: part of one that was not included in the Book of Psalms is found in I Chronicles 16:8ff.

Psalms were chanted, sung and, eventually, read aloud. Taken as a whole, the Book of Psalms presents a picture of God's people at worship that goes far back in time.

Psalms were "modernized" over generations to reflect changing word meanings and styles, just as we do in our hymnals and Bible translations today. As a result we can't easily pick out the oldest psalms from ones composed much later. Favorite phrases and verses from the oldest were probably left exactly as they were in earlier times, as many Christians do with the Lord's Prayer. Other traditional phrases and verses were probably added because a later psalmist loved them.

Psalms and parts of psalms may have been in use even before David's time. Some are his original work or were written to honor him or his son Solomon. Other psalms were seemingly composed during the Babylonian Exile by homesick captives who remembered how much they loved singing and praying them or written in joy by returning exiles who eagerly sought the land their parents left so many years before.

At some point in the assembly process, superscriptions were added to the beginning of many psalms. Their meaning is unclear. We don't know, for example, if a psalm "of David" was written by David, about David, as a tribute to David, or used by David in worship. There are likely some of each. Less than half the psalms have superscriptions and their authors must remain speculative. Styles and subject matter incline us to assign a late date to some, but we'll never know.

Women Psalm Writers?

One fascinating speculation is the possibility that some of the psalms were composed by women. The evidence is entirely indirect, though plausible. We know that women definitely composed hymns and public prayers during the Old Testament time, because some of them are preserved in the Bible. Miriam's Song, discussed above, is the oldest hymn we know about.

Women could be prophets, judges and take other leadership roles in Israelite worship, particularly in the earlier period. In the days of the apostles and the earliest church, women could lead Christian communities, teach and prophecy, as evidenced in the New Testament Book of Acts, the Epistles and much early Christian writing.

In modern Christian hymnody, many of our best hymn writers and translators have been women. This has been the case for centuries. Even though the later church denied women a direct voice in proclaiming God's Word, the Holy Spirit clearly makes use of those gifts in song and poetry. If Mary's Magnificat is any fair example, this was true in Bible times as well.

The Book of Psalms is one place in the Bible where we might find women authors. After all, it isn't as if God withholds conversation with – or inspiration to – women. Christian history amply demonstrates the important gifts God gives the church through its women believers.

In the nature of things, we will probably never know for sure. Still, we can be sure that psalms are God's Word to and from all believers, and may be prayed freely and personally by men and women alike.

St Louis' Psalter, @1260 AD. Illustrations is of Balaam's Prophesy

Christian Content

Psalms is at the center of Christian history. In Luke 24:44 Jesus names the psalter, along with "the Law and the Prophets" as the prophecy that foretells his coming and describes his mission. Early Christian communities used the Book of Psalms in Greek translation as their worship song book and some of the most conservative congregations and some monasteries use them exclusively to this day. Before the invention of printing, hand written copies of the Book of Psalms served as the focus for private prayer and a capsule summary of teaching about God. There is something comforting about using God's own Word in public praise and private worship.

The New Testament quotes psalms repeatedly to show that Jesus' life and ministry was foretold and that he was the Davidic Messiah. Paul quotes psalms to describe God's enemies, their untrustworthiness and deceit (as in Romans 3:13) or the foolishness of human wisdom (1 Cor. 3:20), and so on. Jesus frequently uses psalms, along with the Book of Isaiah, to explain himself and his Father to his followers.

Bible scholar James Luther Mays points out in his essay, "The Forgotten God" that the Psalms' content is oriented toward God, not humans, and that it is in the Book of Psalms that, for Jew and Christian alike, we learn more about who God is, and what God is like than in any other Book of the Bible, "The Psalms themselves, however, contain more direct statements about God than any other book in the two testaments of the Christian canon." (Mays: 29)

It is in Psalms that Israel names and describes the God they worship and testifies to his trustworthiness, love of justice and great mercy. The Christian community found that same Word when they heard God's Praise book.

Organization

The Book of Psalms is organized like a modern hymnal. It collects Israel's favorite psalms and phrases and verses from older psalms into a single document.

The Book of Psalms as we have it today is composed of at least four older and smaller collections. These are:

Psalms 2 — 119 Psalms of the Kingdom of Israel

Probably the original "Book of Praises". The majority are "of David."

Psalms 120—134 Songs of Ascent

These later psalms were probably sung on the annual pilgrimage "up to Jerusalem" for Passover.

Psalms 135— 144 "Old Favorites"

A mixed batch, probably from the Northern Kingdom. They include a few more Psalms of David.

Psalms 145—150 Praise songs used in Temple worship.

Overall, the most favored hymns from various worship communities were collected, their language updated to make them understandable to contemporary worshipers and some additional favorite hymns added.

Structure

Today the Psalter is divided into five "books". This mirrors the "Tanach", the Five Books of the Law of Moses. Perhaps this was done to emphasize that the Book of Psalms is sacred Scripture on a par with the "Law" and the "Prophets".

Some features of the entire book as we have it today:

- Psalm 1 introduces the whole Book of Psalms

- Psalm 150 closes the Psalter with one final Hallelu Yah.

- Psalms 2 and 119 are bookends bracketing an earlier collection.

Inside each of the five "books" are clusters of related psalms:

Book I - Psalms 3-41 - use YHWH (Lord) as the favorite term for God. These hymns may originate in the Southern Kingdom of Judea.

The Book of Psalms
Structure & Organization

Book I

D D D D D D D D D D D D D D D D D D D D D D D D D D

1 2 3 4 5 6 7 8 9/10 11 12 13 14 15 16 17 18 19 20 21 22 23 24 25 26 27 28 29 30 31 32 33 34

AΩ (1) ... AΩ (9/10) ... AΩ (34)

Book II

D D D D D D D K K K K K K A D D D D D D D D D D D D D D C C

35 36 37 38 39 40 41 42 43 44 45 46 47 48 49 50 51 52 53 54 55 56 57 58 59 60 61 62 63 64 65 66 67

AΩ (37)

Book III

D D D S A A A A A A A A A A A K K D K K E E

68 69 70 71 72 73 74 75 76 77 78 79 80 81 82 83 84 85 86 87 88 89

Book IV

M C

90 91 92 93 94

Book V

C C D C D D D D

95 96 97 98 99 100 101 102 103 104 105 106 107 108 109 110 111 112 113 114 115 116 117 118 119 120

AΩ AΩ (111/112) ... AΩ (119)

D D D D D D D D

121 122 123 124 125 126 127 128 129 130 131 132 133 134 135 136 137 138 139 140 141 142 143 144 145 146 147 148 149 150

Songs of Ascents (120–134)

AΩ (145)

Inscriptions

- D David
- S Solomon
- M Moses
- K Sons of Korah
- A Asaph
- E Ezrahites
- C "Psalm" or "Choirmaster"
- ▬ Song of Ascents
- AΩ Acrostic Psalm

Looking at the big picture:

This "library view" identifies various kinds of psalms according to the key in the bottom right.

The width of each psalm roughly indicates its size.

Spaces separate the traditional five Books.

Books II and III prefer to use "Elohim" (God Most High, or God of Gods). These psalms may have roots in the Northern Kingdom of Israel. If so, they give us a glimpse of how the people of God prayed before Jerusalem became the only center of worship.

Fifty-six of the psalms in Books I & II are "Psalms of David". There are a few more in Books III, IV and V.

Book II has many "Songs of the Sons of Korah". These were followers of Korah, a famous Levite chorale leader.

Book III has most of the "Songs of Asaph". Asaph was another Levite chorale leader mentioned in I Chronicles 16:7.

There are two (or three) psalms "of Solomon" and one "of Moses"

Some superscriptions include musical directions or indicate the tune to be used, as probably is the case with "Selah" which may mean a brief pause, or possibly a fanfare from musical instruments.

Regional Variation

Ethiopian Psalter

Psalms was collected in its final form in the late 3rd Century B.C. There are slight differences between Psalters from different traditions.

Already by 200 BC tradition said there were 150 Psalms. To get to that number, the Greek "Septuagint" translation (traditionally called the

LXX) combines Psalms 9 and 10 into one psalm and then splits Psalm 147 in two to bring the number up to 150. LXX also has a 151st Psalm with a superscription "Outside the number".

The Syriac Psalter, in use by Christians and Jews in Iran, Iraq and Syria adds five Aramaic Psalms, included at the end and unnumbered. The psalms that are common to all versions are in the same order and have almost identical wording.

Some translations differ slightly. Psalm 22:16 in the Masoretic text reads "like a lion" instead of "they have pierced my hands and feet". This may be a slip of the pen one way or another — the Hebrew differs by only one letter – or it may indicate an anti-Christian change designed to prevent the psalm's use as a prophecy of Jesus' crucifixion. Most Bibles offer both translations.

Variant readings encourage us to remain humble about whether we know the precise meaning of a text. The Word still gets through.

Hebrew Poetry

The Book of Psalms isn't the only Hebrew poetry in the Scriptures. We've already mentioned Miriam's Psalm" the oldest Hebrew poem, in Exodus 15:21, which may easily date to 1300 BC or earlier, and David's psalm in I Chronicles. In the New Testament, Mary's "Magnificat" is classic Hebrew poetry of a later, more individualistic sort. All such poetry shares a common structure with psalms.

Hebrew poetry translates well into foreign languages. In fact, it translates so well that many believers ascribe this to Divine providence.

The primary characteristic of Bible poetry is parallelism, also found in much other Hebrew writing. Every "line" of a psalm is divided into two parallel half-lines. Half-lines express similar thoughts in different ways, or contrast opposed thoughts:

For example: Psalm 20:7-8

7.   Some trust in chariots and some in horses,

        but we trust in the name of the Lord our God,

8.   They are brought to their knees and fall,

       but we rise up and stand firm."

Parallels may also be "nested" as above, where two lines each contain opposed half-lines, but are parallel to each other. Sometimes a third half line may add to the thought or repeat a thought from another half-line.

We talk about "lines" rather than verses because the Bible was divided into verses much later than when the Book of Psalms was finalized, and the verses don't always correspond with the needs of a particular poem. So some "verses" are half-lines, some are whole lines and some break up lines. Verse structure isn't particularly important when reading a psalm. Don't let it mislead you.

Parallelism is a tremendous aid to interpreting the meaning of a psalm. Philosophers pay much attention to an odd characteristic of human languages: any particular combination of words will have multiple meanings, which are made clear only in context. Every sentence is an approximation. This is inescapable in any language, because if a word had only one precise meaning it would be impossible to create new meaning by combining words!

Hebrew poetry, which pairs each phrase or image with another that says either the same thing or its antithesis, provides its own context to help us figure out which particular meaning is intended. Sacred writing, which we use to guide conduct and to understand God, needs to be broad ranging, so that it applies widely across different life situations, and also unambiguous, so that we don't go off on a wrong tangent because we misunderstand the intent of a passage. Hebrew poetry tends to minimize misunderstanding, even in translation.

Psalms combine into "stanzas" of related lines. Sometimes every stanza begins with the same letter. Other psalms use the next letter of the alphabet for each succeeding line in a stanza. Stanzas make Hebrew easy to memorize and clearly mark related lines.

Gifted translators have sometimes been able to reproduce these poetic elements beautifully, which is one reason the King James Bible is rated one of the masterpieces of English literature. Usually, though, Bible translations aim for exact reproduction of meaning and only suggest the poetry. Look for the lines to keep you straight here.

Psalms in Christian Worship

Christians from the very first devised beautiful ways to use the Psalter in worship. Some congregations read all of a psalm's verses in series. Many emphasize parallelism by reading half lines antiphonally.

Sometimes we recite alternate verses. Elsewhere men read one half-verse, then women read the next in counterpoint. In each case, the custom accentuates the two-line structure of psalms, and also mimics a "God speaks and people answer" model of prayer.

In some Christian traditions all singing during worship is psalms. Psalms are chanted, sung or accompanied by instruments. They are set to Gregorian chant and Calypso rhythm. Christians who do not understand one another's language still share this poetry where beauty is found in images and meaning rather than sound and metre.

Psalms remain perennially appropriate because they name the Lord we worship, and describe the Davidic Messiah. Even though some were a thousand years old when Mary gave birth to the baby Jesus, they speak to the same God, reflect our own problems, doubts, hopes and fears, and deliver the same promise that God has for us today.

Psalm Types

Scholars group psalms by themes, by structure, by how they are written, who is speaking or what the setting is. Looking at related psalms helps bring out their message and lets us see that they are "God's Word". Psalm themes crop up again and again in daily living.

The psalms you prayed at home last week were a sampling of psalm types most often used for Christian devotions. Let's look closely at some less familiar types. Here are some of the Psalm groupings that scholars find interesting and that you may find meaningful for your prayers. There are a few others we will discuss in later sessions.

Acrostic Psalms (e.g. Psalms 2, 9-10, 34, 37, 111, 112, 145)

Each line of an Acrostic Psalm begins with succeeding letters of the Hebrew alphabet, from Aleph to Tav. Psalm 119 is an even more elaborate acrostic – each letter gets a full 8 line stanza where each line starts with the same letter.

This brilliant and difficult achievement is mainly wasted on English readers. Acrostic psalms speak especially to the love the psalmist has for God and the care that went into Hebrew praise. Still, every psalm, even in English, reveals rich imagery and displays the parallelism of Hebrew poetry. And, if you like, you can picture an intent psalm writer searching through his vocabulary for exactly the right phrase that must start with "B", trying to express on parchment the way that all of God's creation fits together as a whole.

Northern Israelite Psalms (e.g. Psalms 45, 77, 80, 81, 133)

"Elohistic" Psalms. These may be older psalms kept by the Northern Kingdom after the United Kingdom split apart. They use "Elohim", literally "God of all Gods" or "Most High God", rather than "YHWH," the Lord who introduced himself to Moses and Abraham, which was the title favored by Temple priests in Jerusalem. Elohistic psalms offer clues to early Israelite poetry and song, and illustrate worship favorites from outside Jerusalem and Judea. Perhaps the Woman at the Well worshiped with these psalms.

Royal Psalms (Psalms 2, 18, 20, 21, 72, 101, 110, 132 and others)

Royal psalms were used when Israel crowned its King, to celebrate a Royal visit, or in worship led by the King. After the Exile and Return, Israel found a broader meaning in these psalms. They pointed the way to the coming Davidic Messiah. Jesus used images from Royal Psalms to reveal God's broader purpose and to explain his own mission and significance. Christians recognized Jesus in the Royal psalms.

Royal psalms were extraordinarily important to Luther. We'll look more closely at the Royal Psalms when we see how Luther prayed the Psalms.

The Lament

The Lament is the basic framework from which almost all psalms are modeled. Laments are also the most numerous psalms. More than half of all psalms are laments. In a Lament, the Psalmist brings a problem to the Lord for resolution.

Most laments share a common structure. The first element is the "complaint", addressed to God. The psalmist can't hear God or see his actions in a situation where God's presence is clearly needed.

Psalm 13 - St. Albans Psalter

After this complaint, the psalmist shares his woes, and then proclaims his innocence, righteousness or faithfulness.

Woes are described vividly. They are almost unendurable to the psalmist. It is often hard to pick out what specifically troubles the psalmist underneath the extravagant language.

The psalmist often mentions more woes than one person is likely to encounter in a lifetime. But the experience of being overwhelmed by our troubles is universal, and familiar to nearly everyone.

Oddly this extravagance helps us use such a psalm to express our own suffering. All troubles have unique elements, but we all experience overwhelming loss, hurt, persecution or isolation and need comforting and support as we try to endure the unendurable.

After the complaint, psalms urge the Lord to act and provide a reason why God should act: because of God's prior saving acts, God's covenant, God's mercy or his justice.

Following this is a request — what the psalmist wants God to do about it all. Sometimes this is the most important part of the psalm. The psalmist has an urgent need and no one but God can help.

Often the psalmist is content to let God decide what to do, only urging him to act swiftly.

Next comes a declaration of trust. Whatever happens, the psalmist vows to wait for God to act, and trusts that God's action, when it comes, will show mercy and love.

Finally the psalmist ends with a word of praise. Sometimes a simple "Praise God" or "Hallelu Yah"; sometimes an entire line or even a whole stanza.

Only the complaint is always present in any particular lament. When an element exists, however, that element is always found in this order:

Complaint
Woes
Reason to act
Request
Trust
Praise

Variations between laments give important glimpses into the purpose of each individual psalm. They reflect what the psalmist feels about God and his situation.

Eadwine the Scribe at Work
—Eadwine Psalter @1160 AD

Psalm 13 - Lament

For the director of music.

A psalm of David.

1. How long, O Lord? Will you forget me forever?
How long will you hide your face from me?

2. How long must I wrestle with my thoughts
and every day have sorrow in my heart?

How long will my enemy triumph over me?

3. Look on me and answer, O Lord my God.
Give light to my eyes or I will sleep in death;

4. my enemy will say, "I have overcome him,"
and my foes will rejoice when I fall.

5. But I trust in your unfailing love;
my heart rejoices in your salvation.

6. I will sing to the Lord,
for he has been good to me.

Thinking About It

• What are the psalmist's complaints?

He can't feel or see God; his enemies seem to be winning and he is running out of strength.

• What does the singer want God to do?

He wants God to reveal himself. Mostly he wants to know God is still there: "Look on me and answer." The psalmist doesn't suggest what God should do, he asks God to be there, and to repair the relationship "for he has been good to me."

Psalm 1 - Wisdom

1 Blessed is the man
who does not walk in the counsel of the wicked

or stand in the way of sinners
or sit in the seat of mockers...

2 But his delight is in the law of the Lord
and on his law he meditates day and night.

3 He is like a tree planted by streams of water,
which yields its fruit in season,

and whose leaf does not wither.
Whatever he does prospers.

4 Not so the wicked!
They are like chaff that the wind blows away.

5 Therefore the wicked will not stand in the judgment,
not sinners in the assembly of the righteous.

6 For the Lord watches over the way of the righteous,
but the way of the wicked will perish.

Thinking About It

• What are the themes you see here?

Some possibilities: The blessings of righteousness; love of the law; God's protective hand, God's justice.

• What are the benefits of righteousness?

Prosperity, delight, stability. The Lord watches over the righteous one.

Wisdom Psalms

Wisdom psalms teach us how to live a righteous life. For a Wisdom writer, God's Law is a joy and blessing. Obedience and faith lead to happiness; wickedness brings suffering. Still the Wisdom writers know this doesn't always happen.

Job, Ecclesiastes, and Psalm 73 are examples of Wisdom writing where obedience doesn't seem to be rewarded. But the psalmist reminds us that God is just and the world's injustice won't last forever.

Set at the beginning of the Book of Psalms, Psalm 1 promises blessings to those who love God and delight in God's Law. This promise is the introduction to the whole Book of Psalms. The psalmist, echoing God's own acts, presents God's gifts first, then moves on to our response.

King David with lyre – Westminster Psalter – 13th Century

King David

Medieval Christian art often presents David as the ideal king for some of the same reasons Jews in Jesus' day looked for a Messiah "like David". Everyone familiar with the Scriptures knows of David's adultery, and his royal and dynastic troubles with his children. However all his human failings were overshadowed by David's love of God and his clear intent to be a "righteous" ruler.

The medieval mind was over familiar with the foibles and folly of kings. Lust, injustice and rebellion were the visible stuff of life in Feudal Europe, as they are today. Only the specifics vary.

Nevertheless, David was a model for the feudal aristocrat. David allowed himself to be critiqued by God, through the prophet Nathan, and he was always ready to turn from doing wrong and try to do right. David's portrait on these psalters is a kind of "statement of intent" on the part of their noble owners.

Today, the Royal Psalms offer us two very different visions that can help us in prayer. First, we can focus on David's obvious delight at the favor he has received from God. This is the man who danced half naked, with the scroll of the Law. A man whom his wife accused of making a fool of himself – for God. Holy Spirit, help us to be like David!

Alongside these visions of David the King, embedded in the rich descriptions of Israel's Royal King, we get a glimpse of what the real "King of Glory" might be like. A king who really is everything that Israel hoped its Davidic King would be. The prayers, the joy, the trust that David gave to God, we can give to the one David calls "Lord", Jesus Christ, the true Davidic Messiah, the real Redeemer.

Psalm 4 – Trust

For the director of music.
With stringed instruments.
A psalm of David.

1 Answer me when I call to you, O my righteous God.
Give me relief from my distress;
be merciful to me and hear my prayer.

2 How long O men, will you turn my glory into shame?
How long will you love delusions and seek false gods?   Selah

3 Know that the Lord has set apart the godly for himself
the Lord will hear when I call to him.

4 In your anger, do not sin when you are on your beds,
search your hearts and be silent.   Selah

5 Offer right sacrifices and trust in the Lord

6 Many are asking, "Who can show us any good?"
Let the light of your face shine upon us, O Lord.

7 You have filled my heart with greater joy
than when their grain and new wine abound.

8 I will lie down and sleep in peace,
for you alone, O Lord, make me dwell in safety.

Thinking About It

• How is this Lament different from Psalm 13?

The speaker complains about his enemies' taunts. He offers advice to those of his hearers who want to be righteous, promises to trust God, and offers thanksgiving for the joy God gives him.

• What are the elements of this psalm?

Request, God indicts evildoers, Wisdom advice, Wisdom question (like Lamentations), Request (repeated), Trust statement.

Psalms of Trust

Psalms of trust move the focus from the complaint to the expression of trust. Sometimes the complaint is completely absent. A Psalm of Trust may speak to the Lord in the third person, as in Psalm 4 and also in Psalm 23, above.

Psalm 4 opens with a "conversation with the Lord" — the petitioner speaks, and God answers. After that, the speaker testifies that God will answer the "many" who ask, "Who can show us any good?" and that God will validate the psalmist's trust.

In Psalm 23 the psalmist envisions God's answer and looks forward to his vindication, though we don't get any sense of who "my enemies" are or what danger he faces from them. The important point is that his Lord is like a protecting shepherd.

Psalms of Trust are especially valuable when life is going well. That is when it's easy to neglect our conversation with God. Remembering to trust and thank God is a wonderful way to deepen our relationship. We learn to see God's hand in the blessings that life continually brings us.

When life is more tangled, Psalms of Trust also have their place. This time, we pray them as a promise, a promise that no matter how bad things seem, we will turn our lives over to God, and trust in God's regard for us.

Trust psalms remind us that God protects, loves and values us, and that our troubles do not really outweigh our blessings. When we remember to declare our trust to God it becomes easier to let our renewed faith shape the rest of our life. With God on our side, we can weather any storm and break through to the clear skies beyond.

Psalm 126 - Songs of Ascent

A song of ascents

1 When the Lord brought back the captives to Zion
we were like men who dreamed

2 Our mouths were filled with laughter,
our tongues with songs of joy.

Then it was said among the nations,
"The Lord has done great things for them."

3 The Lord has done great things for us, and we are filled with joy.

4 Restore our fortunes, O Lord, like streams in the Negev.

5 Those who sow in tears will reap with songs of joy.

6 He who goes out weeping, carrying seed to sow,
will return with songs of joy, carrying sheaves with him.

Thinking About It

• Who are the speakers?

Exiles and their descendants, remembering the return from Babylon.

• What is the psalm's original context?

The end of the Babylonian Captivity, after the journey back to Israel.

• Is it significant that this psalm is a song?

Psalm 126 rejoices, and looks to future joy. Song is the most natural response to overwhelming joy.

• How can Christians use this psalm?

This psalm remembers God's gifts to us and our loved ones. It is an appropriate Easter psalm, or when a family member returns after a long absence.

Songs of Ascent

The best explanation for the 15 "Songs of Ascent" is that they were sung by pilgrims on their three times a year journey "Up to Jerusalem" for the holiday celebrations. The image is of small bands of pilgrims travelling all across Israel as they converge on Jerusalem.

 Other plausible explanations include some or all of:

- They were sung on an "ascendant" (high) musical note.

- They were sung beginning on a low tone, then ascending.

- They were sung by returning Exiles from Babylon.

- They were sung to "elevate" and praise God.

- They were sung while ascending the 15 steps to the Temple inner courtyard.

These psalms may have been written as early as the reign of David or as late as the return from Exile. Four Songs of Ascent are "of David" and one "of Solomon." The rest have no superscription. Songs of Ascent use a slightly different poetic style from most other psalms.

Songs of Ascent repeat key words and phrases throughout the psalm, using them in different ways, interspersed among the lines and stanzas. Repeating phrases carry the main message of the psalm. In Psalm 126 the key phrase is "songs of joy".

The Songs of Ascent collection is arranged as a "journey" from Psalm 120 through 134. Jerusalem means "the house of peace" or "city of peace". In the psalter, the physical journey "Up to Jerusalem" has been spiritualized as a believer's pilgrimage toward the presence of God.

The "journey to God" motif historically appealed to monastic communities. Christian monks and nuns use Songs of Ascent during daily prayer. In Greek Orthodox churches, Songs of Ascent are read on the weekdays of Lent.

Songs of Ascent are good bases for prayers of thanksgiving, of anticipation of coming blessings, and to mark highlights of spiritual journeys.

Psalm 104

1 Praise the Lord, O my soul.
O Lord my God you are very great;

you are clothed with splendor and majesty.

2 He wraps himself in light as with a garment;
he stretches out the heavens like a tent

3 and lays the beams of his upper chambers on their waters.
He makes the clouds his chariot
and rides on the wings of the wind.

4 He makes winds his messengers, flames of fire his servants.

5 He set the earth on its foundations;
it can never be moved.

6 You covered it with the deep as with a garment;
the waters stood above the mountains.

7 But at your rebuke the waters fled,
at the sound of your thunder they took to flight;

8 They flowed over the mountains,
they went down into the valleys,
to the place you assigned for them.

9 You set a boundary they cannot cross;
never again will they cover the earth.

10 He makes the springs pour water into the ravines;
it flows between the mountains.

11 They give water to all the beasts of the field;
the wild donkeys quench their thirst.

12 The birds of the air nest by the waters;
they sing among the branches.

13 He waters the mountains from his upper chambers;
the earth is satisfied by the fruit of his work.

14 He makes grass grow for the cattle,
and brings plants for man to cultivate—
bringing forth food from the earth;

15 wine that gladdens the heart of man,
oil to make his face shine,
and bread that sustains his heart.

16 The trees of the Lord are well watered,
the cedars of Lebanon that he planted.

17 There the birds make their nests;
the stork has his home in the pine trees.

18 The high mountains belong to the wild goats;
the crags are a refuge for the coneys.

19 The moon marks off the seasons,
and the sun knows when to go down.

20 You bring darkness, it becomes night,
and all the beasts of the forest prowl.

21 The lions roar for their prey and seek their food from God.

22 The sun rises and they steal away;
they return and lie down in their dens.

23 Then man goes out to his work,
to his labor until evening.

24 How many are your works, O Lord!
In wisdom you made them all;
the earth is full of your creatures.

25 There is the sea, vast and spacious,
teeming with creatures beyond number –
living things both large and small.

26 There the ships go to and fro,
and the leviathan, which you formed to frolic there.

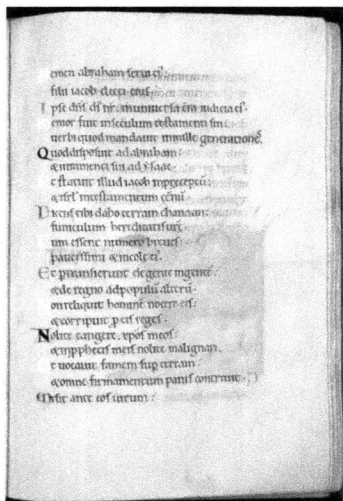

Psalm 104 - St. Albans Psalter – 13th Cent.

27 These all look to you
to give them their food at the proper time.

28 When you give it to them, they gather it up;
when you open your hand,
they are satisfied with good things.

29 When you hide your face, they are terrified;
when you take away their breath, they die and return to the dust.

30 When you send your Spirit, they are created,
and you renew the face of the earth.

31 May the glory of the Lord endure forever;
may the Lord rejoice in his works –

32 He who looks at the earth, and it trembles,
who touches the mountains, and they smoke.

33 I will sing to the Lord all my life;
I will sing praise to my God as long as I live.

34 May my meditation be pleasing to him, as I rejoice in the Lord.

35 But may sinners vanish from the earth and the wicked be no more.

Praise the Lord, O my soul.

Praise the Lord.

Thinking About It

Psalm 104 is one of the longer psalms and so is not prayed so often.

• How does the psalmist use that extra length?

The writer wants to surround you with images, sights and sounds of the work God does every day. His Lord is not absent in heaven.

Instead, God is intimately involved with continually creating and watching over the world he sustains.

- How does Creation History function in praise psalms?

Creation history reminds us that the Lord is a God who continues to create and sustains everyone, every day. He is worthy of praise for more than what he did in the past, or what he might do in the future. Our Lord still looks on his world and, in spite of sin and brokenness, delights in his creation and cares for it lovingly.

- When can we use this prayer?

It is a very good prayer for an extended family worship.

- Is verse 35 a bit jarring?

God promises the New Heaven and Earth will be without sinners or the wicked. Is it presumptuous of us to long for it to happen soon?

The psalmist does not point to personal enemies and ask for their punishment. He asks instead for sinners and "the wicked" to vanish and the earth to belong wholly to God again.

Praise Psalms

Praise psalms are addressed to the Lord God of Israel.

Elements are:

- Call to Praise;

- Attributes or Mighty Deeds of God

- Conclusion.

Psalm 104 elaborates on both God's attributes and deeds. This is rich and beautiful praise for the God who Creates, the God who Sustains, and the God who Saves.

Psalm 150

1 Praise the Lord
Praise God in his sanctuary;
praise him in his mighty heavens.

2 Praise him for his acts of power;
praise him for his surpassing greatness.

3 Praise him with the sounding of the trumpet, praise him with the harp and lyre,
4 praise him with tambourine and dancing, praise him with strings and flute,

5 praise him with the clash of cymbals praise him with resounding cymbals.

6 Let everything that has breath praise the Lord.
Praise the Lord.

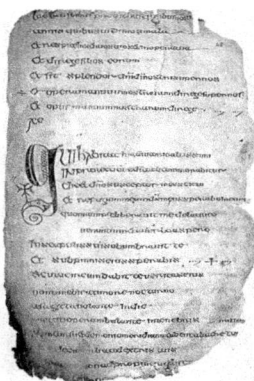

Cathach of Saint Columba – Irish, 6-7th Century

Thinking About It

- How is this different from Psalm 104?

Psalm 150 is pure Praise. There is only one element present here. The psalmist calls on all creation to join him in praise.

- How does it function in the Book of Psalms?

The natural result of all prayer, all song and all worship is that we apprehend how amazing God is. Psalm 150 and the other praise psalms are attempts to put that awe into words.

- How can we use it in prayer?

This is a wonderful prayer for morning or the end of a day. If you are praying the Book of Psalms through from beginning to end, this is the climax. Time to take a deep breath and enjoy the accomplishment.

Book of Psalms — The Great Lament

The entire Book of Psalms fits into the rough form of a Lament. Psalm 1 is the "Introduction" to the whole book, calling the worshiper to righteousness and acknowledging God's power.

Books I and II are full of laments. Israel confesses, pleas for rescue or indicts its enemies. Books III and IV continue the laments and transition into songs of trust and commitment. Psalm 119 ends this early collection with a detailed and loving call to the worshiper to lead a righteous life and trust God's love.

Book V adds the Songs of Ascent with their hopeful note for the future and the Book of Praises ends in a collection of lovely Praise songs.

Psalm 150 brings all creation together for a final Hallelujah.

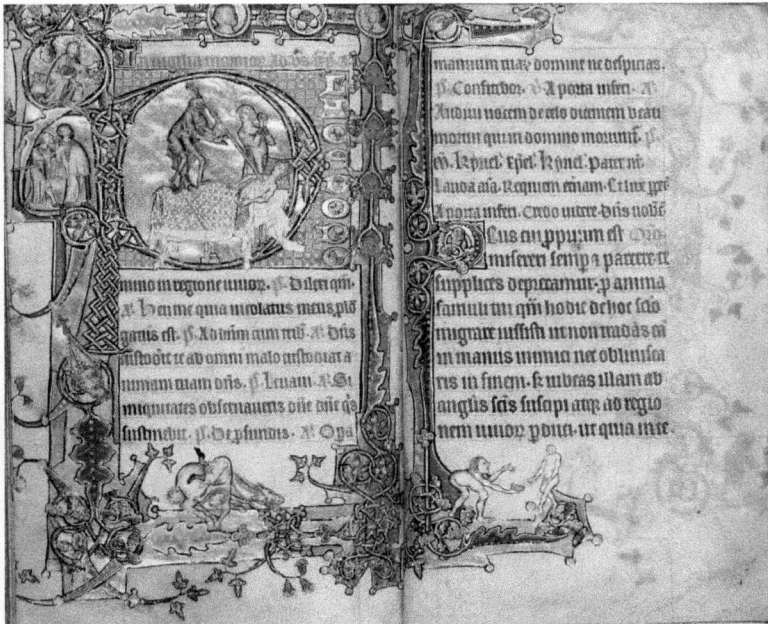

Illustrations of God's wondrous creation from the Macclesfield psalter

Practical Exercise – This Week in Prayer

The psalms you prayed at home for the last chapter were a sampling of several different kinds of psalms: lament, thanksgiving, praise, songs of trust and of ascent. During the next session you will find psalms which strengthen our relationship to God and others which prefigure Christ.

Next – MARTIN LUTHER Reads the Psalms

Martin Luther considered Psalms, "Practically a miniature Bible" and returned to them repeatedly over a long career. He read Psalms as a prophecy of the coming Christ and a guide to our relationship to God, as well as an instruction book about God's Law and God's Grace.

Prayer Psalms

Psalm 2 – A royal psalm of King David

Psalm 8 – How majestic is your name

Psalm 16 – Lord you have assigned me my portion

Psalm 53 – Everyone has turned away

Psalm 58 – Do you rulers speak unjustly?

Thoughts while praying:

- What did Israel think when they sang or prayed these Psalms?
- Did the Exiles hear them differently?
- What about Israel in Jesus time?
- What do Christians hear today?

MARTIN LUTHER READS THE PSALMS

"The Psalter ought to be a dear and beloved book, if only because it promises Christ's death and resurrection so clearly, and so typifies His kingdom and the conditions and nature of all Christendom that it might well be called the little Bible."
                                                                              — Martin Luther

MARTIN LUTHER WAS AN OLD TESTAMENT SCHOLAR. His first serious work concerned the Book of Psalms. He studied the Psalms repeatedly, and published works ranging from six scholarly volumes to a charming piece for his barber, who had asked Martin to teach him to pray:

"A simple way to pray — for Master Peter the Barber."

Dr. Luther focuses on the Book of Psalms' value for Christian worship, the way psalms promise Christ and the way they describe not only the God we trust and worship, but our nature, problems and enemies.

In 1531 Luther wrote "The Summaries of the Psalms". This brief work is an especially accessible aid to daily devotions. In it, Dr. Luther makes clear why Christians should incorporate Psalms into their devotional life. Each psalm, he proposes, includes one or more of five Christian themes to guide us in our prayer life.

Luther's Psalm Types from "Summaries of the Psalms"

Prophecy

Prophetic Psalms make promises to the saints, and give warnings to the Ungodly.

Instruction

What are we to do? What should we avoid in accordance with the Law of God? Psalms of instruction condemn human doctrines and praise the Word of God.

Comfort

These psalms comfort the saints in their tribulations and rebuke tyrants.

Prayer

In which we call on God, praying in all kinds of distress.

Thanks

God is praised and glorified for his blessings and help. This is why the psalter was created, and why it was named the "Book of Praises"

Psalms may express more than one theme, or even contain all at once. These classifications make it easier to understand the psalms and allow us to discern the Word of God for us contained inside.

Luther's Prayer Advice

from "A simple way to pray – for Master Peter the Barber"

Luther prayed daily as a foundation for his life. Here are some snippets of Luther's advice to Master Peter (and us).

"If I have only two hours, I pray for one hour. If I am in more of a hurry, I pray longer."

"It is a good thing to let prayer be the first business of the morning and the last thing at night."

"You should know that I do not want you to recite all these words in prayer. That would make it idle chatter and prattle."

"It is of great importance that the heart be made ready and eager for prayer."

Luther's Seal

Martin Luther (1535) – Lucas Cranach the Elder

"With practice one can take the Ten Commandments one day, a psalm or chapter of Holy Scripture the next day and use them as flint and steel to kindle a flame in the heart."

"Pray daily, except in real emergencies."

"Use Psalms, the Lord's Prayer, the Ten Commandments, Creed, the Holy Scriptures."

"Make room for good thoughts, even when it means you don't finish a whole psalm."

Psalm 2 - a Royal Psalm

1 Why do the nations conspire
and the peoples plot in vain?

2 The kings of the earth take their stand
and the rulers gather together against the Lord
and against his Anointed One.

3 "Let us break their chains," they say,
"and throw off their fetters."

4 The one enthroned in heaven laughs;
the Lord scoffs at them.

5 Then he rebukes them in his anger
and terrifies them in his wrath, saying

6 I have installed my King on Zion, my holy hill."

7 I will proclaim the decree of the Lord:
He said to me, "you are my Son,
today I have become your Father.

8 Ask of me, and I will make the nations your inheritance,
the ends of the earth your possession.

9 You will rule them with an iron scepter;
you will dash them to pieces like pottery."

10 Therefore you kings, be wise;
be warned, you rulers of the earth.

11 Serve the Lord with fear
and rejoice with trembling.

12 Kiss the Son, lest he be angry
and you will be destroyed in your way,
for his wrath can flare up in a moment.

Blessed are all who take refuge in him.

Thought Questions

- Who is the psalmist talking about?

This psalm was originally sung when a new King was crowned, or perhaps on the occasion of a royal visit.

- Does the message change between the time of David and the early Christians?

Christians were clear that Jesus is the real Messianic King.

- Is this image of the Christ as powerful ruler disquieting?

We don't spend much time thinking about Jesus as an absolute ruler, the King of Glory, in spite of our confession that "he will come again, to judge the living and the dead." Perhaps we should.

- Which of Luther's themes does this contain?

Background Information

This is a "Royal Psalm", written for the coronation of a Davidic king. It presents a picture of a king supported by God and confident of the Lord's favor, able to defy the surrounding powers. This king, God declares, becomes not only the "son of David", but the "Son of God" – God says, "today I have become your Father."

In time, the people of God saw this as a prophecy of the coming Messianic King, the idealized ruler beloved of God, whom God will task with displaying God's power and glory to the nations.

Christians used this psalm to interpret Jesus' ministry as its startling fulfillment. These phrases also describe the future reign of Christ, where Jesus' suffering, death and resurrection finally reverses the sinfull order and opens the way into God's future Kingdom in a new heaven and new earth.

Verse 7 establishes the prophecy fulfilled at the River Jordan, when John baptizes Jesus and God's voice from heaven declares, "This is my beloved Son."

The New Testament Book of Revelation has similar imagery with Jesus separating the sheep from the goats. Christ also uses the language of power in the Gospels (e.g. Matthew 25: 31ff).

Our experience teaches us that no human can be safely trusted with this kind of power, not even King David. God's only Son is a whole different level of King.

What did Luther have to say about Psalm 2?

"Psalm 2 is a prophecy of Christ, that he would suffer and through his suffering become King and Lord of the whole world.

This psalm flows from the first commandment, in which God promises to be our God, who will help us in every trouble and will work all good for us – just as he has, through Christ, delivered us from sin, death and hell and brought us to eternal life."

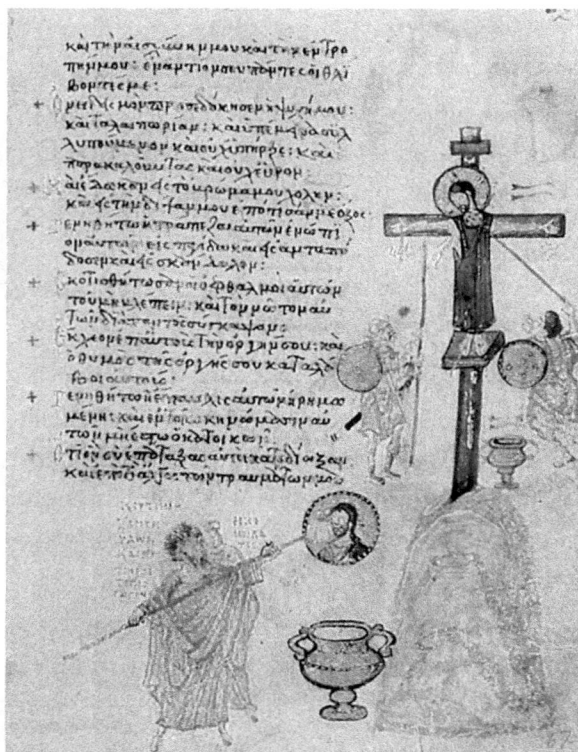

Crucifixian scene
– Chludov Psalter

Psalm 8 - the son of man

1 O Lord, our Lord,
how majestic is thy name in all the earth!

You have set your glory
above the heavens.

2 From the lips of children and infants
you have ordained praise

because of your enemies,
to silence the foe and the avenger.

3 When I consider your heavens,
the work of your fingers,

the moon and the stars
which you have set in place,

4 what is man that you are mindful of him,
the son of man that you care for him?

5 You made him a little lower than the heavenly beings
and crowned him with glory and honor.

6 You made him ruler over the works of your hands;
you put everything under his feet:

7 all flocks and herds, and the beasts of the field,

8 the birds of the air, and the fish of the sea,
all that swims the paths of the seas.

9 O Lord, our Lord,
how majestic is your name in all the earth.

Thought Questions

- Jesus liked to call himself the Son of Man. The translation above doesn't capitalize the phrase, implying that the psalmist isn't talking about the Messiah. Does this seem right?

- Does the meaning change for Christians?

The psalmist seems to be thinking about a representative of "mankind". Jesus is the archetype, the one man who can safely be made "ruler over the works of your hands".

- Which of Luther's themes does this contain?

Background Information

This is another "Royal Psalm", which introduces the Davidic King as the "son of man". It confesses God's supreme sovereignty over all creation and assigns the son of man dominion over the earth as a mark of God's special regard, not as a right, but as a gift.

The answer to the Psalm's question, "what is man that you are mindful of him?" is different if you are considering Jesus or human kind in general. The next verse, "You made him a little lower than the heavenly beings, and crowned him with glory and honor" can be distracting. Jesus is not "a little lower than the heavenly beings." Early Christians explained that Jesus voluntarily shed his divinity for a time, becoming "a little lower" in order to reconcile us to God.

On the superscription: one possible translation of, "according to gittith", is "according to 'The young lady from Gath'". Gath was an "outsider" or enemy city to Israel. Nobody knows what the provenance of the tune is or even for sure what this direction means. If this is a popular country song repurposed for worship, it reminds me of Luther's reply when chided for the tavern ditty to which he set one of his hymns, "Why should the devil have all the good tunes?"

What did Luther have to say about Psalm 8?

"Psalm 8 is a prophecy of Christ—his sufferings, resurrection and kingly rule over all creatures. This kingdom shall be established by the voice of children, that is, it will be established not by sword or armor but by Word and faith alone. It reminds us of the 1st Commandment, that God intends to be our God, and the 2nd petition of the Lord's Prayer."

Psalm 16 - Keep me safe, O God

1 Keep me safe, O God,
for in you I take refuge.

2 I said to the Lord, "You are my Lord;
apart from you I have no good thing."

3 As for the saints who are in the land,
they are the glorious ones in whom
is all my delight.

4 The sorrows of those will increase
who run after other gods.

I will not pour out their libations of blood
or take up their names on my lips.

5 Lord, you have assigned me my portion and my cup;
you have made my lot secure.

6 The boundary lines have fallen for me in pleasant places;
surely I have a delightful inheritance.

7 I will praise the Lord, who counsels me;
even at night my heart instructs me.

8 I have set the Lord always before me.
Because he is at my right hand, I will not be shaken.

9 Therefore my heart is glad and my tongue rejoices;
my body also will rest secure,

10 because you will not abandon me to the grave,
nor will you let your Holy One see decay.

11 You have made known to me the path of life;
you will fill me with joy in your presence,
with eternal pleasures at your right hand.

Thinking About It

- What are the reasons the psalmist praises the Lord?

God has "made known to me the path of life".

- What promises does the speaker make?

He "takes refuge", "will not be shaken", "rests secure"

- What do Christians find in this psalm?

During the Christian era, Jesus' promise of eternal life for believers transformed the way this psalm was heard.

- Which of Luther's themes does this contain?

Background

This is a Davidic psalm of thanksgiving. The psalmist makes a vow to trust in the Lord, and gives thanks for blessings received and blessings anticipated. The overtones of Christ's suffering and death, the references to pouring out the blood, the cup, and the claim that God will not abandon the speaker to the grave make this an irresistible prophecy of Christ.

Perhaps the psalmist is a foreigner in the act of choosing Israel's Lord, YHWH, to be his own Lord. Read this way, with the speaker as a new believer, the psalm is an especially beautiful praise poem where the speaker looks forward to his new life as a servant of the God who can be trusted. Whoever its author, psalm 16 shows how the Word of the Lord reaches deeply into many different lives.

What did Luther have to say about Psalm 16?

"Psalm 16 is a prophecy of the sufferings and resurrection of Christ, as the apostles themselves powerfully indicate (Acts 2:25 and 13:35). It clearly gives witness that Christ has discarded as idolatry the old law with its sacrifices and worship and has chosen other saints and another people to be his heirs. It reminds us of the 2nd and 3rd Commandments and the 2nd petition of the Lord's Prayer."

Psalm 53 - Everyone has turned away

For the director of music.
 According to mahalath.
A maskil of David.

1 The fool says in his heart,
"There is no God".

They are corrupt, and their ways are vile
there is no one who does good.

2 God looks down from heaven
on the sons of men to see if there are any who understand,
any who seek God.

3 Everyone has turned away,
they have together become corrupt;

there is no one who does good,
not even one.

4 Will the evildoers never learn –
those who devour my people as men eat bread
and who do not call on God?

5 There they were, overwhelmed with dread,
where there was nothing to dread.

God scattered the bones of those who attacked you;
you put them to shame, for God despised them.

6 Oh, that salvation for Israel would come out of Zion!
When God restores the fortunes of his people,
let Jacob rejoice and Israel be glad!

Thinking About It

- This psalm acknowledges that the speaker is not "one who does good", but who hopes for God's promised salvation anyway.

It is almost, but not quite, a psalm of despair. Perhaps the last line of the last verse is the lesson here.

- Is this appropriate for today?

Modern Christians who encounter indifference, scorn and even violence in some countries can empathize with this psalmist who hopes God will come soon, and put things right.

- Which of Luther's themes does this psalm contain?

Background

Psalm 53 is probably an older psalm. Psalm 14 is nearly identical except that God is addressed with the Sacred Name YHWH (Lord). In Psalm 53 he is "Elohim" (God Most High or God of Gods). This is somewhat like the two versions of "A Mighty Fortress", both written by Luther, both important in different Lutheran traditions.

The small difference between the two psalms is thought provoking. Psalm 14 is a prophecy against those who mistreat the poor. "You evildoers frustrate the plans of the poor, but the Lord is their refuge."

Psalm 53 reminds the believer that God has rescued them, "God scattered the bones of those who attacked you; you put them to shame, for God despised them." Each psalm addresses itself to different hearers.

What did Luther have to say about Psalm 53?

"The 53rd Psalm is a psalm of instruction and a prophecy like the 14th psalm. Both have nearly the same verses and words.

In brief, both of them rebuke the faithless work-saints, who prosecute the true doctrine and the true teachers.

At the end, it proclaims the Gospel and the kingdom of Christ, who shall come out of Zion."

Psalm 58

For the director of music.
To the tune of "Do not destroy."
Of David. A miktam.

1 Do you rulers indeed speak justly?
Do you judge uprightly among men?

2 No, in your heart you devise injustice,
and your hands mete out violence on the earth.

3 Even from birth, the wicked go astray;
from the womb they are wayward and speak lies.

4 Their venom is like the venom of a snake,
like that of a cobra that has stopped its ears,

5 that will not heed the tune of the charmer,
however skillful the enchanter may be.

6 Break the teeth in their mouths, O God;
tear out, O Lord, the fangs of the lions!

7 Let them vanish like water that flows away;
when they draw the bow, let their arrows be blunted.

8 Like a slug melting away as it moves along,
like a stillborn child, may they not see the sun.

9 Before your pots can feel the heat of the thorns –
whether they be green or dry – the wicked will be swept away.

10 The righteous will be glad when they are avenged,
when they bathe their feet in the blood of the wicked.

11 Then men will say, "Surely the righteous are still rewarded;
surely there is a God who judges the earth."

Thinking About It

•   Who are the psalmist's enemies?

Unjust rulers, judges.

•   Is it ever appropriate to ask for God's judgment?

Jesus calls for us to "love our enemies". Yet it is appropriate to hope for the Day of the Lord when wickedness will be abolished and humans will be "made right" with God. Righteous hate would seem to be a step too far.

•   Which of Luther's themes does this contain?

Background

The psalmist calls out the rulers and powerful for their injustice, violence and lies. He then calls on God to thwart their plans, turn their wicked intentions to equally violent fates and justify the righteous faithful. By this men will know "Surely the righteous still are rewarded; surely there is a God who judges the earth."

Verse 9 is obscure. The meaning may be "in less time than it takes to heat a pot, whether with green or dry wood."

What did Luther have to say about Psalm 58?

"The 58th Psalm is a psalm of comfort against the stiff-necked teachers who stubbornly carry through with their error, stop up their ears and never let themselves be corrected, but rather threaten to devour the godly."

"The psalmist comforts himself, using five comparisons, that they will not carry out their intentions — yes, that they will not accomplish half of them......"

".....Though all these are intended to be great and proceed with success, nevertheless nothing shall come from them."

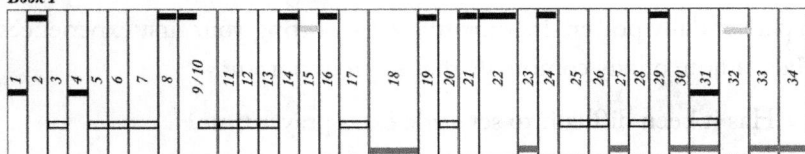

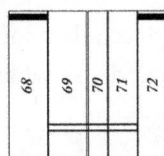
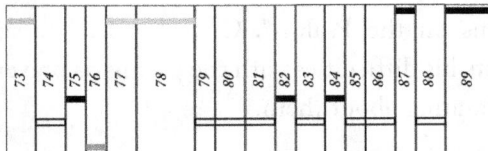
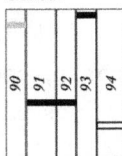

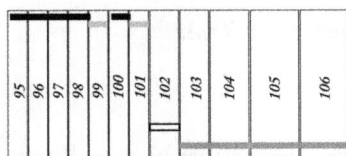
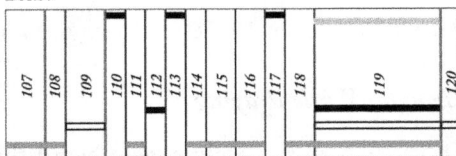

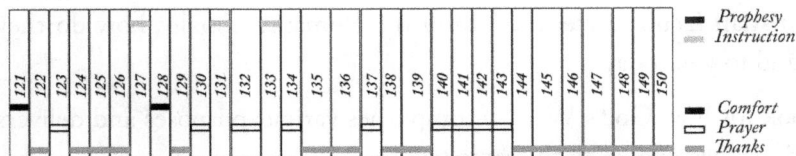

Each Psalm is annotated according to Luther's categories.
A psalm can and often does belong to more than one category.
The apparent width of the psalm roughly indicates its size.

Practical Exercise – Progress Report

At this point we have had two weeks of using a common set of psalms as part of daily prayer. Its time to start reporting your first experiences. Make a note of any comments that seem important:

- Has it been difficult to set aside extra prayer time?

- Have the psalms meshed well with your regular prayer life?

- Do the psalms suggest new prayer issues and topics?

- Did you have difficulty relating the psalms to contemporary concerns?

Next C. S. LEWIS reads the psalms

In "Reflections on the Psalms", C. S. Lewis, Christian scholar and layman, reports his difficulties with the psalms as prayers, and also what he finds exhilarating about them.

Prayer Psalms:

Psalms 36, 137, 6, 19, 50 – Cursings, Judgment and Trust

Thoughts While Praying

Consider how the psalms were heard throughout Bible history. Picture someone from David's time, then one who heard Jesus' teaching, or a Christian facing persecution from the Romans. Finally, how do they sound to you today?

Look for how God's Word accomplishes various purposes and delivers various messages with the same text.

- Do some psalms seem unChristian? Why or why not?

- What parts of these psalms prepare early believers for the coming Messiah?

- What lessons are aimed at modern Christians today?

C. S. LEWIS REFLECTS

"I write for the unlearned about things in which I am unlearned myself. "

"If an excuse is needed (and perhaps it is) for writing such a book, my excuse would be something like this. It often happens that two schoolboys can solve difficulties in their work better than the master can. "

"The fellow pupil can help more than the master because he knows less. The difficulty we want him to explain is one he has recently met. The expert met it so long ago that he has forgotten."

C. S. LEWIS, SOMEWHAT UNEXPECTEDLY, HAS BECOME a rich source of theological insight for the modern Christian of our generation. Though Lewis does not claim special training or theological insight, his ability to clearly see, and plainly state, difficulties and challenges that all believers face is widely admired. Today, his writing is read throughout English-speaking Christianity. Possibly because he was a convert later in life, Lewis has a knack for reflecting the doubts and questions that come up as we try to live a Christian life.

In additiion to his writing, Lewis, in person, was a brilliant raconteur..

In "Reflections on the Psalms", published in 1958, Lewis questions — and tentatively answers — the difficulties and worries that occur to him when he confronts the Psalms. His thoughts, which cover ground mostly familiar to thoughtful Christians, encourage us to conduct an honest dialog with God.

The five psalms we prayed last week bring up specific difficulties and insights that Lewis comments on. His thoughts are linked to the most relevant psalm.

Lewis' remarks are not definitive "answers to the quiz". Still less are they received wisdom to be copied or memorized. Instead, Lewis offers his thoughts to us from one experienced Christian to another, for you to think about.

Great learning is not identical to great theological understanding – that is a gift of the Holy Spirit. But insights, when they come, can and should be shared. God uses ordinary people to make the Good News plain, as God used this thoughtful man to stimulate talking to God.

Psalm 36 - Judgment

For the director of music
Of David the servant of the Lord.

1 An oracle is within my heart
concerning the sinfulness of the wicked:
There is no fear of God before his eyes.

2 For in his own eyes he flatters himself
too much to detect or hate his sin.

3 The words of his mouth are wicked and deceitful;
he has ceased to be wise and do good.

4 Even on his bed he plots evil;
he commits himself to a sinful course
and does not reject what is wrong.

5 Your love, O Lord, reaches to the heavens
your faithfulness to the skies.

6 Your righteousness is like the mighty mountains,
your justice like the great deep.

7 How priceless is your unfailing love!
Both high and low among men
find refuge in the shadow of your wings.

8 They feast on the abundance of your house;
you give them drink from your river of delights.

9 For within you is the fountain of life;
in your light, we see light.

10 Continue your love to those who know you,
your righteousness to the upright in heart.

11 May the foot of the proud not come against me,
nor the hand of the wicked drive me away.

12 See how the evildoers lie fallen –
thrown down, not able to rise!

Thought Questions

• What does the psalmist consider the sins of the wicked?

• Which of God's characteristics impresses the psalmist most?

• The psalmist welcomes – calls for – God's judgment day. Is this something you are comfortable praying for?

Lewis on Judgment

Here is part of an extended meditation on innocence and guilt:

"If there is any thought at which a Christian trembles it is the thought of God's "judgment".

"It was therefore with great surprise that I first noticed how the Psalmists talk about the judgments of God. They talk like this:

> *"O let the nations rejoice and be glad,*
> *for thou shalt judge the folk righteously."*

"In the Bible, God's "Judges" are more like "Champions" of the powerless than lawgivers."

"The Christian sees himself as a defendant in a Criminal case. The Christian is in court against his will. He is looking for mercy, not justice."

"The Psalmist sees himself as the plaintiff in a civil suit. He can't get his case heard. He looks for justice instead of injustice."

"It is possible to be unrighteous, and yet be innocent on a particular issue. It is not unreasonable to hope God will "hear your case" and protect you from injustice even if you yourself sin."

"Reflections on the Psalms" pp 10–14

Psalm 50 - Humility and Righteousness

A psalm of Asaph.

1 The Mighty One, God, the Lord,
speaks and summons the earth

from the rising of the sun to the
place where it sets.

2 From Zion, perfect in beauty,
God shines forth.

3 Our God comes and will not be silent;
a fire devours before him,
and around him a tempest rages.

4 He summons the heavens above,
and the earth, that he may judge his people:

5 "Gather to me my consecrated ones,
who made a covenant with me by sacrifice."

6 And the heavens proclaim his righteousness,
for God himself is judge.   Selah

7 "Hear, O my people, and I will speak,
O Israel, and I will testify against you:

I am God, your God.

8 I do not rebuke you for your sacrifices
or your burnt offerings, which are ever before me.

9 I have no need of a bull from your stall
or of goats from your pens,

10 for every animal of the forest is mine,
and the cattle on a thousand hills.

11 I know every bird in the mountains,
and the creatures of the field are mine.

12 If I were hungry I would not tell you,
for the world is mine, and all that is in it.

13 Do I eat the flesh of bulls
or drink the blood of goats?

14 Sacrifice thank offerings to God,
fulfill your vows to the Most High,

15 and call upon me in the day of trouble;
I will deliver you, and you will honor me."

16 But to the wicked, God says:
"What right have you to recite my laws
or take my covenant on your lips?

17 You hate my instruction
and cast my words behind you.

18 When you see a thief, you join with him;
you throw in your lot with adulterers.

19 You use your mouth for evil
and harness your tongue to deceit.

20 You speak continually against your brother
and slander your own mother's son.

21 These things you have done and I kept silent;
you thought I was altogether like you.
But I will rebuke you and accuse you to your face.

22 Consider this, you who forget God,
or I will tear you to pieces, with none to rescue;

23 He who sacrifices thank offerings honors me,
and he prepares the way so that I may show him the salvation of God."

Thinking About It

•   What is the setting for Psalm 50?

This is really a sermon. God speaks to the gathered people of Israel.

•   Who is God talking to?

God speaks to people who believe themselves righteous because they do all the sacrifices and know the law well.

•   What does God look for?

God's charge to Israel is "sacrifice and fulfill your vows". Sacrifice isn't enough by itself. God asks for a state of mind, an attitude. "Prepare the way so that I may show him the salvation of God."

Lewis on Humility and Righteousness before God

"There are, indeed, some passages in which the psalmist approaches Christian humility and wisely lose their confidence."

"It is important to make a distinction: between the conviction that one is in the right, and the conviction that one is 'Righteous'. Since none of us is righteous, the second is always a delusion."

"But any of us may be, probably all of us at one time or another are, in the right about some particular issue. What is more, the worse man may be in the right against the better man."

"The question whether the disputed pencil belongs to Tommy or Charles is quite distinct from the question which is the nicer little boy."   *"Reflections on the Psalms" p17*

Psalm 137 - the Curses

1 By the rivers of Babylon we sat and wept
when we remembered Zion

2 There on the poplars
we hung our harps.

3 for there our captors asked us for songs.
our tormentors demanded songs of joy;
they said, "Sing for us one of the songs of Zion!"

4 How can we sing the songs of the Lord
while in a foreign land?

5 If I forget you O Jerusalem,
may my right hand forget its skill.

6 May my tongue cling to the roof of my mouth
if I do not remember you,
if I do not consider Jerusalem my highest joy.

7 Remember, O Lord, what the Edomites did
on the day Jerusalem fell.
"Tear it down," they cried, "tear it down to its foundations!"

8 O Daughter of Babylon, doomed to destruction,
happy is he who repays you for what you have done to us –

9 he who seizes your infants
and dashes them against the rocks.

Thinking About It

• What is the psalmist's complaint?

The singer feels desolate and bitter about the destruction of Jerusalem. The exiles are victims of injustice and the psalmist wants vengeance.

• What is asked of the Lord?

The singer wants God to avenge what has been done to his people. In Jeremiah 50, God proclaims that, although he used Babylon to chastise Israel, Babylon itself will be judged for its wickedness and found wanting. Babylon, after all, chose to behave wickedly when God withdrew his protection from Israel.

• What do you think about the curses in verses 8—9?

We're not hearing only God's thoughts in Psalm 137. Instead, we're overhearing an honest conversation with God.

The psalmist is overcome by grief and rage and loss. God's answer is found in other psalms, in other parts of the Bible, and in Jesus' life, death and resurrection. God invites us to trust him with the full fury of our emotions. He will answer, and he will bring peace, and justice.

Lewis on the Curses

"In the 23rd psalm, for example, the Lord "preparest a table before me, in the presence of mine enemies".

"The poet's enjoyment of his present prosperity would not be complete unless those horrid Joneses (who used to look down their noses at him) were watching it all, and hating it."

"In some of the psalms the spirit of hatred which strikes us in the face is like the heat from a furnace mouth".

"It is monstrously simple-minded to read the cursings in the psalms with no feelings except one of horror at the uncharity of the poets. They are indeed devilish. But we must also think of those who made them so. Their hatreds are the reactions to something. Such hatreds are the kind of thing that cruelty and injustice, by a kind of natural law, produce.

"This, among other things, is what wrong-doing means. Take from a man his freedom or his goods and you may have taken his innocence, almost his humanity, as well. Not all victims go and hang themselves like Mr. Pilgrim; they may live and hate."

"Reflections on the Psalms" pages 20–21, 25; Psalm 23:5, KJV.

Psalm 6 -on Death

For the director of music
With stringed instruments
According to sheminith
A psalm of David

1 O Lord, do not rebuke me in your anger
 or discipline me in your wrath.

2 Be merciful to me, Lord, for I am faint;
O Lord, heal me for my bones are in agony.

3 My soul is in anguish.
How long, O Lord, how long?

4 Turn, O Lord, and deliver me;
save me because of your unfailing love.

5 No one remembers you when he is dead.
Who praises you from the grave?

6 I am worn out from groaning;
all night long I flood my bed with weeping
and drench my couch with tears.

7 My eyes grow weak with sorrow;
they fail because of all my foes.

8 Away from me all you who do evil,
for the Lord has heard my weeping.

9 The Lord has heard my cry for mercy;
the Lord accepts my prayer.

10 All my enemies will be ashamed and dismayed;
they will turn back in sudden disgrace.

Thinking About It

•   Why does the psalmist believe God should answer his prayer?

The poet is suffering and can't hold out much longer. If he dies, God will have one less worshiper.

•   Is the writer asking for vengeance?

The psalmist asks for mercy and for the Lord to hear and act.

•   What is the psalmist's view of death?

Death is the end of everything; there is no intimation of an afterlife.

Lewis on Death

"It seems quite clear that in most parts of the Old Testament there is little or no belief in a future life; certainly no belief that is of any religious importance."

"The word translated 'soul' in our versions of the Psalms means simply 'life'; the word translated "hell" means simply 'the land of the dead', the state of all the dead, good and bad alike, Sheol."

"For the truth seems to me to be that happiness or misery beyond death, simply in themselves, are not even religious subjects at all. A man who believes in them will of course be prudent to seek the one and avoid the other. But that seems to have no more to do with religion than looking after one's health or saving money for one's old age....."

"God is not in the center. He is still important only for the sake of something else......"

It is surely, therefore, very possible that when God began to reveal himself to men, to show them that he, and nothing else, is their true goal and the satisfaction of their needs, and that he has a claim on them simply by being what He is, apart from anything he can bestow or deny, it may have been absolutely necessary that this revelation should not begin with any hint of future Beatitude or Perdition.

These are not the right points to begin at. *"Reflections" p.36, 39–40.*

Psalm 19 - Loving the Law

For the director of music.
A psalm of David.

1 The heavens declare the glory of God;
the skies proclaim the work of his hands.

2 Day after day they pour forth speech;
night after night they display knowledge.

3 There is no speech or language
 where their voice is not heard.

4 Their voice goes out into all the earth,
their words to the ends of the world.
In the heavens he has pitched a tent for the sun,

5 which is like a bridegroom coming forth from his pavilion,
like a champion rejoicing to run his course.

6 It rises at one end of the heavens
and makes its circuit to the other;
nothing is hidden from its heat.

7 The law of the Lord is perfect, reviving the soul.
The statutes of the Lord are trustworthy, making wise the simple.

8 The precepts of the Lord are right, giving joy to the heart.
The commands of the Lord are radiant, giving light to the eyes.

9 The fear of the Lord is pure, enduring forever.
The ordinances of the Lord are sure, and altogether righteous.

10 They are more precious than gold, than much pure gold;
they are sweeter than honey, than honey from the comb.

11 By them is your servant warned;
in keeping them is great reward.

12 Who can discern his errors?
Forgive my hidden faults.

13 Keep your servant also from willful sins;
may they not rule over me.

Then will I be blameless,
innocent of great transgression.

14 May the words of my mouth and the meditation of my heart
be pleasing in your sight,

O Lord, my Rock and my Redeemer.

Thinking About It

•   To what is the singer comparing creation?

Creation is awe inspiring, like the Torah.

•   What is the psalmist asking from God?

That God forgive his faults and keep him from great error.

Lewis on loving the Law

"But I think we see pretty well what the Psalmists mean. They mean that in the Law they find the "real" or "correct" or "stable", well-grounded, directions for living. ...There are many rival directions for living, as the Pagan cultures all around us show. When the poets call the directions or "rulings" of Jahweh "true" they are expressing the assurance that these, and not those others, are the "real" or "valid" or unassailable ones; that they are based on the very nature of things and the very nature of God."

"By this assurance they put themselves, implicitly, on the right side of a controversy which arose far later among Christians. There were in the Eighteenth Century terrible theologians who held that "God did not command certain things because they are right, but certain things are right because God commanded them.....

Such a view makes God a mere arbitrary tyrant. It would be better and less irreligious to believe in no God and to have no ethics than to believe in such a God and to have such a theology as this."

"The Jews of course never discuss this in abstract and philosophical terms. But at once, and completely, they assume the right view...

They know that the Lord (not merely obedience to the Lord) is "righteous" and commands "righteousness" because He loves it. He enjoins what is good because it is good, because He is good. Hence His laws have "emeth" - Truth - intrinsic validity, rock-bottom reality, being rooted in His own nature, and are therefore as solid as that Nature which he has created."

"Reflections on the Psalms" pages 60 – 61

Practical Exercise – Progress Report

At this point, we have used three sets of psalms for daily devotional prayer, and reflected on their meaning in company with Martin Luther and C. S. Lewis.

*   Has it been difficult to set aside prayer time?

*   Have psalms prayers meshed well with your regular prayer life?

*   Have the psalms suggested new issues and topics for your prayers?

*   Did you have any difficulty relating the psalms you prayed to contemporary concerns?

*   Did praying the Book of Psalms make the psalms more accessible?

Next —DIETRICH BONHOEFFER reads the psalms

In "Psalms, Prayerbook of the Bible", pastor, conspirator and martyr Dietrich Bonhoeffer explores one source of his inspiration.

Prayer Psalms

41, 25, 70, 37, 97 – Psalms of Desperation and Hope

Thoughts While Praying

*   Consider how the psalms were heard throughout Bible history.

Look for ways God accomplishes various purposes with the same text.

*   Do parts of these psalms seem unChristian?

Do they reflect a different relationship with God? Do the troubles of the psalmist warp their faith?

*   What parts of these psalms foreshadow Christ?

These psalms describe what God is like. Jesus shows us what "God with us" is like. Together Psalms and the Gospels help us to look for God's presence in the right places and recognize God's nearness in the lonliness of our troubles.

Psalms discussed in Dietrich Bonhoeffer's "Psalms, Prayerbook of the Bible"

Psalms are listed by topic. Some psalms appear several times.

Creation:
> 8, 19, 29, 105

Law:
> 1, 19, 119

Holy History:
> 78, 105, 106

Messiah:
> 2, 20, 21, 22, 45, 69, 72, 110

Church:
> 15, 23, 27, 42, 46, 48, 50, 63, 81, 84, 87, 137

Life:
> 37, 65, 103

Suffering:
> 13, 31, 35, 38, 41, 44, 54, 55, 56, 61, 74, 79, 86, 88, 102, 105

Trust:
> 23, 37, 63, 73, 91

Guilt:
> 6, 14, 15, 25, 31, 32, 38, 39, 40, 41, 51, 69, 102, 130, 143

Enemies:
> 5, 7, 9, 10, 13, 16, 21, 23, 28, 31, 35, 36, 40, 41, 44, 52, 54, 55, 58, 59, 68, 69, 70, 71, 137

End of Days:
> 2, 16, 17, 49, 56, 73, 90, 96, 97, 98, 102, 110, 118, 148, 149, 150.

DIETRICH BONHOEFFER
– PSALMS IN THE TIME OF CRISIS

IN THE 1930'S, DR. DIETRICH BONHOEFFER WAS THE leading Lutheran theologian of the Confessional Church. He was head of an underground Seminary formed to resist Nazi efforts to co-opt Christianity. By 1939 he found himself in New York, in an overseas call arranged to keep him out of the hands of the Gestapo. He spent several months in New York, finding spiritual comfort in, among other places, black churches in Harlem, whose enthusiasm he admired.

Meanwhile, the situation in Germany worsened. Sometime in late summer, Bonhoeffer made an immensely fateful decision. As he explained to friend and fellow theologian Reinhold Neibuhr,

"I have come to the conclusion that I made a mistake in coming to America. I must live through this difficult period in our national history with the people of Germany. I will have no right to participate in the reconstruction of Christian life in Germany after the war if I do not share the trials of this time with my people... Christians in Germany will have to face the terrible alternative of either willing the defeat of their nation in order that Christian civiliza-tion may survive or willing the victory of their nation and thereby destroying civilization. I know which of these alternatives I must choose but I cannot make that choice from security."

During the same period, while Bonhoeffer was immersed in passive resistance to the Nazis and personally wrestling with what contribution he could make to the state of Christianity in Germany, he wrote a tiny volume, "Das Gebetbuch der Bibel" which was published in 1940.

Reading Psalms as a Subversive Document

Bonhoeffer's book, a brief review of the Book of Psalms as a Christian prayer resource was a subversive act in Germany in 1940. His book unmistakably underlined the inseparable unity of Jewish history and the Christian faith. The Gestapo took notice. Bonhoeffer was called in for questioning. He explained that, as a scholarly work, his book was not subject to prior review by Nazi authorities. In any case, he said, it had nothing whatever to do with current politics.

This was yet another act of resistance. By this time Bonhoeffer felt he owed the Nazis no commitment to the truth. His evasion kept him out of prison but he was warned against publishing anything at all in the future without Gestapo review and approval.

"Psalms, Prayerbook of the Bible" was not translated and published in English until the 1960's, well after memories of the predicament of Christians in pre-WWII Germany had receded into the past. Today his book attracts new generations of Christian readers interested in a modern look at Bible based prayer. In "Psalms" Bonhoeffer underscores the deep connection between Christians speaking to God, inspired by the Holy Spirit, and God's written Word in Scripture, which both produce spiritual insights and answers them.

Psalms as Commentary on Life

Bonhoeffer's work connects with modern readers in a different way. It shows that even in our stressful and eventful lives, we can draw closer to God using God's own prayer book as a conduit for our fears and God's reassurance.

Dietrich Bonhoeffer used psalms as his lifeline to God. Back in Germany, for example, he went to great lengths to acquire a scholarly work solely about Psalm 119. He had heard this was "the most boring psalm" and wished to explore it while he still had freedom to do so.

Psalms were Bonhoeffer's refuge from, and God's commentary on, the current events in which Bonhoeffer was inextricably enmeshed. They refreshed his faith and replenished his trust in God's power and love.

We are unlikely to find ourselves in waters as deep as those in which Dietrich Bonhoeffer was forced to swim. Many of us nevertheless find ourselves in over our heads. For us, psalms can be a life preserver by re-connecting us with the God who alone can save.

Bonhoeffer – Lord, Teach Us to Pray

"And so we must learn to pray. The child learns to speak because his father speaks to him. He learns the speech of his father. So we learn to speak to God because God has spoken to us and speaks to us. By means of the speech of the Father in heaven his children learn to speak with him. Repeating God's own words after him, we learn to speak to him. We ought to speak to God and he wants to hear us, not in the false and confused speech of our heart, but in the clear and pure speech which God has spoken to us in Jesus Christ."

"God's speech in Jesus Christ meets us in the Holy Scriptures. If we wish to pray with confidence and gladness, then the words of the Holy Scripture will have to be the solid basis of our prayer. For here we know that Jesus Christ, the Word of God, teaches us to pray. The words which come from God become, then, the steps on which we find our way to God."

Bonhoeffer, "Psalms, the Prayerbook of the Bible" page 11

Bonhoeffer – Learning to Pray

"It is at first very surprising that there is a prayer book in the Bible. The Holy Scripture is the Word of God to us. But the prayers are the words of men. How do prayers then get into the Bible? Let us make no mistake about it, the Bible is the Word of God even in the Psalms.

Then are these prayers to God also God's own word? That seems rather difficult to understand. We grasp it only when we remember that we can learn true prayer only from Jesus Christ, from the word of the Son of God, who lives with us men, to God the Father, who lives in eternity.... In his mouth the word of man becomes the Word of God, and if we pray his prayer with him, the Word of God becomes once again the word of man.

Bonhoeffer, "Psalms, the Prayerbook of the Bible" page 13

Dietrich Bonhoeffer - 1939

Prayer Psalms

Consider the questions and thoughts that come up as you pray the psalms. As we have done with Luther and C. S. Lewis, we will look at what Dietrich Bonhoeffer has to say and compare what he found in the psalms to the Word that you heard in your own prayer.

Psalm 41

For the director of music.
A Psalm of David.

1 Blessed is he who has regard for the weak;
the Lord delivers him in times of trouble.

2 The Lord will protect him and preserve his life;
he will bless him in the land
and not surrender him to the desire of his foes.

3 The Lord will sustain him on his sickbed
and restore him from his bed of illness.

4 I said "O Lord, have mercy on me;
heal me, for I have sinned against you."

5 My enemies say of me in malice,
"When will he die and his name perish?"

6 Whenever one comes to see me,
he speaks falsely, while his heart gathers slander;
then he goes out and spreads it abroad.

7 All my enemies whisper together against me;
they imagine the worst for me, saying,

8 "A vile disease has beset him;
he will never get up from the place where he lies."

9 Even my close friend, whom I trusted,
he who shared my bread,
has lifted up his heel against me.

10 But you, O Lord, have mercy on me;
raise me up, that I may repay them.

11 I know that you are pleased with me,
for my enemy does not triumph over me.

12 In my integrity you uphold me
and set me in your presence forever.

13 Praise be to the Lord, the God of Israel,
from everlasting to everlasting.

Amen and Amen.

Illuminated "D", Ingeborg Psalter

Thinking About It

•   What would these psalms have said to you, in Bonhoeffer's situation during 1939 and 1940?

Bonhoeffer's latest biography by Eric Metaxis, "Bonhoeffer: Pastor, Martyr, Prophet, Spy", conveys some of the stress, suspicion and danger of these years. From our relatively peaceful vantage point, we probably need help imagining how hemmed in and hunted Bonhoeffer felt, even before he resolved to resist Hitler actively.

•   Do the psalms still speak to you in 2013?

I have never been hunted by a suspicious government and abandoned by peers who thought me too dangerous to associate with. No one considers me a dangerous radical. That Bonhoeffer found refuge in the psalms is sobering. Psalms are a reminder that God will sustain, no matter how bad things get.

Bonhoeffer on the Laments

"These Psalms give us permission to bring our deepest worries boldly to God.

Bonhoeffer in Prison

"Serious illness and severe loneliness before God and men, threat, persecution, imprisonment, and whatever conceivable peril there is on earth are known by the Psalms....."

"Because it happens with God's will, indeed because God knows it completely and knows it better than we ourselves, only God himself can help. But therefore also must all our questions again and again assault God himself."

"There is in the Psalms no quick and easy resignation to suffering. There is always struggle, anxiety, doubt...."

"But even in the deepest hopelessness, God alone remains the one addressed...."

"The wrathful God is confronted countless times with his promise, his previous blessings, the honor of his name among men.... "

"There are no theoretical answers in the Psalms to all these questions, as there are none in the New Testament. The only real answer is Jesus Christ. But this answer is already sought in the Psalms. It is common to all of them that they cast every difficulty and agony on God: "We can no longer bear it, take it from us and bear it yourself, you alone can handle suffering." That is the goal of all the lamentation Psalms."

Bonhoeffer, "Psalms, the Prayerbook of the Bible" pp. 46–48.

Psalm 25

Of David.

1 To you, O Lord, I lift up my soul;

2 in you I trust, O my God.
Do not let me be put to shame,
nor let my enemies triumph over me.

3 No one whose hope is in you will ever be put to shame.
but they will be put to shame who are treacherous without excuse.

4 Show me your ways, O Lord, teach me your paths;

5 guide me in your truth and teach me,
for you are God my savior, and my hope is in you all day long.

6 Remember, O Lord, your great mercy and love,
for they are from of old.

7 Remember not the sins of my youth and my rebellious ways;
according to your love remember me, for you are good, O Lord.

8 Good and upright is the Lord;
therefore he instructs sinners in his ways.

9 He guides the humble in what is right
and teaches them his way.

10 All the ways of the Lord are loving and faithful
for those who keep the demands of his covenant.

11 For the sake of your name, O Lord,
forgive my iniquity, though it is great.

12 Who, then is the man that fears the Lord?
He will instruct him in the way chosen for him.

13 He will spend his days in prosperity,
and his descendants will inherit the land.

14 The Lord confides in those who fear him;
he makes his covenant known to them.

15 My eyes are ever on the Lord,
for only he will release my feet from the snare.

16 Turn to me and be gracious to me,
for I am lonely and afflicted.

17 The troubles of my heart have multiplied;
free me from my anguish.

18 Look upon my affliction and my distress
and take away all my sins.

19 See how my enemies have increased
and how fiercely they hate me!

20 Guard my life and rescue me;
let me not be put to shame, for I take refuge in you.

21 May integrity and uprightness protect me,
because my hope is in you.

22 Redeem Israel, O God,
from all their troubles!

Thinking About It

- What did this psalm say to Dietrich Bonhoeffer?

The last verse is telling. The psalmist is moved as much by concern for his people as for his personal troubles.

- What do they say to you in 2013?

Bonhoeffer on Sin and Repentance

"The Psalmist knows he, and his people, sin and are sinners.

"It is an abbreviation and an endangering of Christian prayer if it revolves exclusively around the forgiveness of sins. There is such a thing as the confident leaving behind of sin for the sake of Jesus Christ. Yet in no way does the Psalter omit the prayer of repentance. The seven so-called repentance Psalms (6, 32, 38, 51, 102, 130, 143), but not only they (also Psalms 14, 15, 25, 31, 39, 40, 41 and others) lead us into the total depth of the recognition of sin before God. They lead us to the confession of guilt and direct our complete confidence to the forgiving grace of God, so that Luther has quite correctly called them the "Pauline Psalms". "

"Usually a special occasion leads us to such a prayer. It is serious guilt (Psalms 32 and 51) or an unexpected suffering that drives to repentance (Psalms 38 and 102). In every case, all hope is fixed on free forgiveness as it has been offered to us and promised by God in his word about Jesus Christ for all times."

Bonhoeffer, "Psalms, the Prayerbook of the Bible" pp. 50-51.

Psalm 70

For the director of music
Of David. A petition.

1 Hasten, O God to save me;
O Lord, come quickly to help me.

2 May those who seek my life
be put to shame and confusion;

may all who desire my ruin
be turned back in disgrace.

3 May those who say to me, "Aha!, aha!"
turn back because of their shame.

4 But may all those who seek you
rejoice and be glad in you.

may those who love your salvation always say,
"Let God be exalted!"

5 Yet I am poor and needy;
come quickly to help me, O God.

You are my help and my deliverer;
O Lord, do not delay.

Thinking About It

- What did this psalm say to Bonhoeffer?

- What do they say to you in 2013?

- What can we make of the Psalms that call down the wrath of God on the unrighteous?

Bonhoeffer on Judgment

"The enemies referred to here are enemies of the cause of God, who lay hands on us for the sake of God. It is therefore nowhere a matter of personal conflict. Nowhere does the one who prays these psalms want to take revenge into his own hands. He calls for the wrath of God alone (Romans 12:19). ....This means that only the one who is himself innocent in relation to his enemy can leave the vengeance to God. The prayer for the vengeance of God is the prayer for the execution of his righteousness in the judgment of sin. This judgment must be made public if God is to stand by his word.....I myself with my sin, belong under this judgment. I have no right to want to hinder this judgment. It must be fulfilled for God's sake and it has been fulfilled, certainly, in wonderful ways....."

"God's vengeance did not strike the sinners, but the one sinless man who stood in the sinner's place, namely God's own Son. Jesus Christ bore the wrath of God for the execution of which the psalm prays. He stilled God's wrath toward sin and prayed in the hour of the execution of the divine judgment: "Father, forgive them, for they do not know what they do!"....

"That was the end of all phony thoughts about the love of God which do not take sin seriously. God hates and redirects his enemies to the only righteous one, and this one asks forgiveness for them. Only in the cross of Jesus is the love of God to be found....."

"I pray the imprecatory psalms in the certainty of their marvellous fulfillment. "

Bonhoeffer, "Psalms, the Prayerbook of the Bible" page 58-59.

Psalm 37

Of David.

1 Do not fret because of evil men
or be envious of those who do wrong;

2 for like the grass they will soon wither,
like green plants they will soon die away.

3 Trust in the Lord and do good;
dwell in the land and enjoy safe pasture.

4 Delight yourself in the Lord
and he will give you the desires of your heart.

5 Commit your way to the Lord;
trust in him and he will do this:

6 He will make your righteousness shine like the dawn,
the justice of your cause like the noonday sun.

7 Be still before the Lord and wait patiently for him;
do not fret when men succeed in their ways,
when they carry out their wicked schemes.

8 Refrain from anger and turn from wrath;
do not fret – it leads only to evil.

9 For evil men will be cut off,
but those who hope in the Lord will inherit the land.

10 A little while, and the wicked will be no more;
though you look for them, they will not be found.

11 But the meek will inherit the land
and enjoy great peace.

12 The wicked plot against the righteous
and gnash their teeth at them;

13 but the Lord laughs at the wicked,
for he knows their day is coming.

14 The wicked draw the sword and bend the bow
to bring down the poor and needy,
to slay those whose ways are upright.

15 But their swords will pierce their own hearts,
and their bows will be broken.

16 Better the little the righteous have
than the wealth of many wicked;

17 for the power of the wicked will be broken,
but the Lord upholds the righteous.

18 The days of the blameless are known to the Lord,
and their inheritance will endure forever.

19 In times of disaster they will not wither;
in days of famine they will know plenty.

20 But the wicked will perish:
the Lord's enemies will be like the beauty of the fields,
they will vanish – vanish like smoke.

21 The wicked borrow and do not repay,
but the righteous give generously;

22 those the Lord blesses will inherit the land,
but those he curses will be cut off.

23 If the Lord delights in a man's way,
he makes his steps firm;

24 though he stumble, he will not fall,
for the Lord upholds him with his hand.

25 I was young and now I am old,
yet I have never seen the righteous forsaken
or their children begging for bread.

26 They are always generous and lend freely;
their children will be blessed.

27 Turn from evil and do good;
then you will dwell in the land forever.

28 For the Lord loves the just
and will not forsake his faithful ones.

They will be protected forever,
but the offspring of the wicked will be cut off;

29 the righteous will inherit the land
and dwell in it forever.

30 The mouth of the righteous man utters wisdom,
and his tongue speaks what is just.

31 The law of his God is in his heart;
his feet do not slip.

32 The wicked lie in wait for the righteous,
seeking their very lives;

33 but the Lord will not leave them in their power
or let them be condemned when brought to trial.

34 Wait for the Lord and keep his way.
He will exalt you to inherit the land;
when the wicked are cut off you will see it.

35 I have seen a wicked and ruthless man
flourishing like a green tree in its native soil,

36 but he soon passed away and was no more;
though I looked for him, he could not be found.

37 Consider the blameless, observe the upright;
there is a future for the man of peace.

38 But all sinners will be destroyed;
the future of the wicked will be cut off.

39 The salvation of the righteous comes from the Lord;
he is their stronghold in time of trouble.

40 The Lord helps them and delivers them;
he delivers them from the wicked and saves them,
because they take refuge in him.

Icon - First Council of Nicea

Thinking About It

*   What did this psalm say to Bonhoeffer?

*   What do they say to you in 2013?

*   Is it presumptuous to ask for the blessings of life?

Bonhoeffer on blessings

"Precisely at the point where men must make many sacrifices in following Jesus, as did the disciples, they will answer, "Nothing!" to the question of Jesus, "Did you lack anything?" (Luke 22:35) The presupposition to this is the insight of the Psalms: "Better is the little that the righteous has than the abundance of the many wicked" (Psalm 37:16).

"Therefore we need not have a bad conscience when we pray with the Psalter for life, health, peace and earthly goods if we only recognize, as do the Psalms themselves, that all of this is evidence of the gracious fellowship of God with us, and we thereby hold fast to the fact that God's gifts are better than life."

Bonhoeffer, "Psalms, the Prayerbook of the Bible" pages 44-45

Psalm 97

1 The Lord reigns, let the earth be glad;
let the distant shores rejoice.

2 Clouds and thick darkness surround him;
righteousness and justice are the foundation of his throne.

3 Fire goes before him
and consumes his foes on every side.

4 His lightning lights up the world
the earth sees and trembles.

5 The mountains melt like wax before the Lord,
before the Lord of all the earth.

6 The heavens proclaim his righteousness,
and all peoples see his glory.

7 All who worship images are put to shame,
those who boast in idols –
worship him, all you gods!

8 Zion hears and rejoices
and the villages of Judah are glad because of your judgments, O Lord.

9 For you, O Lord, are the Most High over all the earth;
you are exalted far above all gods.

10 Let those who love the Lord hate evil,
for he guards the lives of his faithful ones
and delivers them from the hands of the wicked.

11 Light is shed upon the righteous
and joy on the upright in heart

12 Rejoice in the Lord, you who are righteous,
and praise his holy name.

Illuminated "B" St. Louis Psalter

Thinking About It

•   What did this psalm say to Bonhoeffer?

•   What does it say to you?

•   Does psalm 97 foreshadow Jesus' – and our – resurrection?

Bonhoeffer on Resurrection and the Life to Come

"The hope of Christians is directed to the return of Jesus and the resurrection of the dead. In the Psalter this hope is not expressed literally. That which since the resurrection of Jesus has divided itself in the church into a long line of events of holy history toward the end of all things is, from the viewpoint of the Old Testament, still a single indivisible unity. Life in fellowship with the God of revelation, the final victory of God in the world, and the setting up of the messianic kingdom are objects of prayer in the psalms."

"To be sure, the psalms request fellowship with God in earthly life, but they know that this fellowship is not completed in earthly life, but continues beyond it, even stands in opposition to it. (Psalm 17:14). So life in fellowship with God is already on the other side of death."

"Death is to be sure the irrevocable bitter end for body and soul. It is the wages of sin, and the remembrance of it is necessary (Psalms 39 and 90). On the other side of death, however is the eternal God (Psalms 90 and 102). Therefore not death but life will triumph in the power of God."

Bonhoeffer, "Psalms, the Prayerbook of the Bible" psalm 61-62

Practical Exercise – Reflection and Reporting

Reporting our experiences

In the upcoming session the main focus will be on using skills and insights you have developed here for your personal meditation.

Look over your experience praying the Psalms. What advice could you give now? What would you do differently?

The final psalms remind us of some of the topics we covered. We also relate some stories about various Christians over the centuries who encountered the Psalms and had the experience change their lives.

Every contact with the Bible is another opportunity to tell the Christian story and to encourage each other towards a deeper and richer faith life. I hope you will take these strengthened skills and let God take a stronger place in your life.

Prayer Psalms:

Psalm 22

Jesus' words on the Cross. Psalm 22 was Jesus' cry of anguish, his declaration of trust, and God's promise to his disciples.

Psalm 10

Why, O Lord, do you stand far off?

Psalm 15

What does God require of us?

Psalm 24

Luther calls this is a prophecy of Christ, the coming King of Glory.

Psalm 118

Jesus quotes this Psalm to teach his disciples who he was. Dietrich Bonhoeffer clung to it as a guarantee that the evil days would someday pass. It makes a superb "thank you" to God for his blessings.

PRAYING THE PSALMS – THE BIG PICTURE

Our goals for this class were:

•   Explore how God uses, and answers, prayer.

•   Present a variety of psalms for your personal prayer life.

•   Look at the role psalms play in Christian worship.

In this process, we combined selected psalms with your accustomed prayers. Everyone was encouraged to give these psalms a close reading and apply them to your individual concerns. This session, our task is to reflect how it all went.

Looking at the Process

Here are some suggested questions to get things started.

•   How is praying with psalms different from your usual prayers?

•   Are the Psalmist's concerns similar to your own?

•   Did the psalms uncover things you wouldn't normally bring to prayer?

•   What did you find different about praying with the psalms compared to your usual prayer style?

•   Were Martin Luther, C. S. Lewis and Dietrich Bonhoeffer's insights helpful to you? Which ones, and why?

Psalms through the Ages

Possibly the Christian thinkers who have been exploring the psalms with us were a bit intimidating. Who are we to expect God to make our lives over in the way Martin Luther's or Dietrich Bonhoeffer's or C. S. Lewis' lives were changed? Aside from taking refuge in Jesus' assurance that God, who watches over every sparrow, cares about us too, let's look at a few more examples of the way that God's Word, working through the Book of Psalms, changes lives and strengthens faith.

Prayer Review

We'll go through last week's psalms together as a sort of graduation exercise. We also will take a closer look at how various other people have used psalms to structure their prayers.

If you have a prayer partner, write down anything interesting that either of you brings up. This is one of the major benefits prayer partners can bring to private prayer – allowing your partner's creative insight and imagination to stimulate your own thoughts.

Psalm 22

1 My God, my God, why have you forsaken me?
Why are you so far from saving me,
so far from the words of my groaning?

2 O my God, I cry out by day, but you do not answer,
by night, and am not silent.

3 Yet you are enthroned as the Holy One;
you are the praise of Israel.

4 In you our fathers put their trust;
they trusted and you delivered them.

5 They cried to you and were saved;
in you they trusted and were not disappointed.

6 But I am a worm and not a man,
scorned by men and despised by the people.

7 All who see me mock me;
they hurl insults, shaking their heads:

8 "He trusts in the Lord;
let the Lord rescue him.
let him deliver him, since he delights in him."

9 Yet you brought me out of the womb;
you made me trust in you even at my mother's breast.

10 From birth I was cast upon you;
from my mother's womb you have been my God.

11 Do not be far from me, for trouble is near,
and there is no one to help.

12 Many bulls surround me;
strong bulls of Bashan encircle me.

13 Roaring lions tearing their prey
open their mouths wide against me.

14 I am poured out like water,
and all my bones are out of joint.

my heart has turned to wax;
it has melted away within me.

15 My strength is dried up like a potsherd,
and my tongue sticks to the roof of my mouth;
you lay me in the dust of death.

16 Dogs have surrounded me;
a band of evil men has encircled me,
they have pierced my hands and my feet.

17 I can count all my bones;
people stare and gloat over me.

18 They divide my garments among them
and cast lots over my clothing.

19 But you, O Lord, be not far off;
O my Strength, come quickly to help me.

20 Deliver me from the sword,
my precious life from the power of the dogs.

21 Rescue me from the mouth of the lions;
save me from the horns of the wild oxen.

22 I will declare your name to my brothers,
in the congregation I will praise you.

23 You who fear the Lord, praise him!
All you descendants of Jacob, honor him!
Revere him, all you descendants of Israel!

24 For he has not despised or disdained
the suffering of the afflicted one;

he has not hidden his face from him
but has listened to his cry for help.

25 From you comes the theme of my praise in the great assembly;
before those who fear you will I fulfill my vows.

26 The poor will eat and be satisfied;
they who seek the Lord will praise him –
may your hearts live forever!

27 All the ends of the earth will remember and turn to the Lord,
and all the families of the nations will bow down before him,

28 for dominion belongs to the Lord
and he rules over the nations.

29 All the rich of the earth will feast and worship;
all who go down to the dust will kneel before him –
those who cannot keep themselves alive.

30 Posterity will serve him;
future generations will be told about the Lord.

31 They will proclaim his righteousness to a people yet unborn –
for he has done it.

Thinking About It

- Psalm 22 is Jesus' cry of anguish, his declaration of trust, and God's promise to believers, all in one.

- Have you experienced desolation in your life?

- Were you still able to hope?

Jesus' prayer from the Cross.

Philip Yancey is a popular writer in Christian education circles. A big part of his appeal is that he is our contemporary and faces many of the same problems and opportunities we encounter daily. In his book "The Bible Jesus Read" he discusses how unfamiliar he was with the Book of Psalms and how reluctant to use it for personal devotions.

Over time he came to realize that Psalms is a look "over the shoulder" of Israelite believers as they talk to God. Their conversation is a living example of the relationship God wants us to have with Him. Even the difficult parts. He discovered psalms could enliven his prayer, too.

Along the way he recounts the story of the Soviet dissident Anatoly Shcharansky who was imprisoned in Siberia for 13 years. During that time, his lifeline was a battered copy of the Psalms in Hebrew. Praying and reading psalms gave him the strength to endure, with difficulty, privations and trials that we would have trouble imagining.

As Shcharansky's wife puts it,

> "In a lonely cell in Chistopol prison, locked alone with the Psalms of David, Anatoly found expression for his innermost feelings in the outpourings of the King of Israel thousands of years ago."

(Yancey: 120)

Psalms is not a one-note feel good Bible lesson. Psalm writers plead with God, rage at God, question God and, surprisingly sometimes, rejoice with God. All the range of human feelings goes into these songs and prayers, and all the hopes of God's people are expressed, beautifully. These, unless you are already a poet, are the words you wish you could use to talk to God. These, even if you are a poet, are words that can shape your heart, as they strengthened Jesus' heart in the middle of his suffering on the Cross.

You and I will, by the Grace of God, never face a lonely cell, far from friends and family. Psalms have the power to reach into desolation like that. They can even reach farther; they can reach into the depths of all human weakness, sin and isolation.

Psalm 22 is an absolutely riveting prophecy of Jesus' torment on the cross, filled with minor details like the ones in verses 16 – 18 which revealed to early Christians that they were in the presence of God's chosen one. The psalm is full of agonizing images of suffering. After Golgotha, the disciples realized the dying Jesus was Isaiah's Suffering Servant and David's forsaken believer from Psalm 22. Jesus' dying quote — the first verse of Psalm 22 — is powerful evidence that he also knew this and accepted the burden of the world's sin.

God's Word continues forth until it accomplishes all its purposes, including reminding the dying Son of God who he was and what was at stake there on the Cross.

Psalm 24

Of David. A psalm.

1 The earth is the Lord's, and everything in it,
the world, and all who live in it;

2 for he founded it upon the seas,
and established it upon the waters.

3 Who may ascend the hill of the Lord?
Who may stand in his holy place?

4 He who has clean hands and a pure heart,
who does not lift up his soul to an idol,
or swear by that which is false.

5 He will receive blessing from the Lord
and vindication from God his Savior.

6 Such is the generation of those who seek him,
who seek your face, O God of Jacob.

7 Lift up your heads, O you gates;
be lifted up, you ancient doors,
that the King of glory may come in.

8 Who is this King of glory?
the Lord strong and mighty,
the Lord mighty in battle.

9 Lift up your heads O you gates;
lift them up, you ancient doors,
that the King of glory may come in.

10 Who is this King of glory?
the Lord Almighty –
he is the King of glory.   Selah

Thinking About It

- This song for King David foreshadows the true King of Glory
- Israel's hope is a portrait of our Redeemer

Extended meditation

Psalms 22, 23 and 24 taken together and in order make a good long meditation on God's promise, the cross Jesus bore for us, and what God requires of us. The trilogy takes you through the Valley of the Shadow of Death, and out the other side to God's Holy Hill where the Suffering Servant opens the door.

Psalters

After the political collapse of Rome, education became an expensive luxury not available to most of the populace. Manuscripts were hand lettered on parchment or leather, and they were very expensive. Producing a Bible might take a team of monks an entire year.

Most people in cities, towns and in the countryside learned God's story through plays, parades and sermons. Even the minor clergy might themselves have memorized rather than read the Holy Offices which they performed. What playlets, parades and puppet shows lacked in precision they made up for in immediacy and entertainment value. But for all who could read, or could afford it, access to the scriptures was a prize avidly sought after.

For the wealthy noble, bishop or royal patron, or a community of monks and nuns in an abbey, manuscripts of the Book of Psalms, with perhaps a copy of the Lord's Prayer and the Apostle's Creed, had to suffice. If the copyist or someone else was artistically talented, these Psalters, or Breviaries, would be illustrated with scenes from Bible history, pictures of the Saints or perhaps a patron or local notable.

Such Psalters were useful because cloistered communities typically recited the psalms several times a day, going through the entire 150 in a week. Because of their great artistic value, their spiritual, and in time their historical value, a number of psalters survive.

One of the most beautiful is the St. Albans Psalter, now housed in Switzerland. In a very rare happenstance, a manuscript biography of its original owner, Christina of Markyate, who in her lifetime grew into a local saint of some note, has also survived. Christina's story is a look at how God enriches a believer's life in unusual ways using the power of prayer and the psalms to grow faith and stimulate religious imagination.

Illuminated "C" from St. Albans Psalter – believed to show Christina of Markyate

Psalms of Liberation

Christina of Markyate was, her biographer tells us, a pretty Saxon girl who was born somewhere around 1096 AD in England, just north of St. Albans Abbey, which was then a popular destination for pilgrimages. As a child she made a personal vow to be a nun, but as in modern romances, her parents were determined she marry instead.

She ran away from this arranged marriage on her wedding night. Through various churchly connections (she had half-siblings who were children of the local bishop) she managed to hide from her parents in the cells of various local hermits – some of whom proved safer than others.

After several years of this perilous existence, she came under protection of the elderly Roger the Hermit, an erstwhile monk of St. Albans Abbey in his cell at Markyate. She tended him for some time. When he died the Abbot of St. Albans allowed her to take over Roger's cell and thereafter provided food and protection for her.

We don't know exactly what her schooling had been, but apparently she could read and write. Over the course of years her imaginative devotions, including daily recitation of psalms, creeds and prayer common to the monastic orders, plus a series of personal visions that grew out of this daily contemplation, led the Abbot to decide that she was a trustworthy conduit to the thoughts of God.

With time Christina played an increasing role in the spiritual life of the monks, or at least the Abbot, with her meditations and visions. This led to some jealousy on the part of the monks, although the relationship, as detailed by Christina, her biographer and Abbot Geoffrey's testimony, was chaste throughout.

This is plausible enough given her history, her determination to seek a religious vocation, and her biographer's apparent willingness to graphically relate her youthful sexual perils while she was hiding from her parents and under "protection" of various churchmen before Roger the Hermit took her in.

From this distant vantage point, it looks like Abbot Geoffrey realized that while he might have been an excellent administrator and leader, Christina had more spiritual insight and imagination, and valued her accordingly.

Abbot Geoffrey was a former schoolmaster, and at some point, while the monks were preparing an illuminated psalter for their own use, he decided that it should be, instead, a gift to Christina for her personal devotions. The result was a lovely manuscript that survives today.

A careful examination of the St. Albans psalter indicates ways the original design was subtly altered to meet Christina's spiritual needs. In the later psalms, the "Alexis Master" — the principal artist – depicted many more scenes of Christ's interactions with women than in the first portion. There is also a single illuminated letter, a "C", that seems to be a portrait of Christina in this part of the St. Albans psalter.

Christina outlived Geoffrey by several years, remaining a spiritual advisor to the monks of St. Albans until her death sometime after 1155 AD. By the time of her death, pilgrims were visiting St. Albans not only as a saint's shrine and the site of Roger the Hermit's former abode, but also to see and hear Christina. Christina became a local saint and, her biographer tells us, was canonized under the name Saint Theodora, which literally is a feminine form of "God-worshiper" or "God-lover".

The St. Albans Psalter, Christina's memories of stories from the Bible, her religious visions sparked by those memories, and her reading, seem to have become great spiritual assets to the monks of St. Albans and the surrounding countryside.

This modestly educated (as far as we can tell) young woman was able, by meditation and religious imagination, to carve an independent, fulfilling life for herself out of the rather difficult set of choices available for women of her station in the High Middle Ages.

Christina's prayers built a life full of faith, visions and thoughts of God. God's gifts can be an astonishingly personalized fit for our talents and our calling.

Psalm 10

1 Why, O Lord, do you stand far off?
Why do you hide yourself in times of trouble?

2 In his arrogance the wicked man hunts down the weak,
who are caught in the schemes he devises.

3 He boasts of the cravings of his heart;
he blesses the greedy and reviles the Lord.

4 In his pride the wicked does not seek him;
in all his thoughts there is no room for God.

5 His ways are always prosperous,
he is haughty and your laws are far from him;
he sneers at all his enemies.

6 He says to himself, "Nothing will shake me.
I'll always be happy and never have trouble."

7 His mouth is full of curses and lies and threats;
trouble and evil are under his tongue.

8 He lies in wait near the villages;
from ambush he murders the innocent,
watching in secret for his victims.

9 He lies in wait like a lion in cover;
he lies in wait to catch the helpless;
he catches the helpless and drags them off in his net.

10 His victims are crushed, they collapse;
they fall under his strength.

11 He says to himself, "God has forgotten;
he covers his face and never sees."

12 Arise, Lord! Lift up your hand, O God.
Do not forget the helpless.

13 Why does the wicked man revile God?
Why does he say to himself,
"He won't call me to account"?

14 But you, O God, do see trouble and grief;
you consider it to take it in hand.

The victim commits himself to you;
you are the helper of the fatherless.

15 Break the arm of the wicked and evil man;
call him to account for his wickedness
that would not be found out.

16 The Lord is King for ever and ever;
the nations will perish from his land.

17 You hear, O Lord, the desire of the afflicted;
you encourage them, and you listen to their cry,

18 Defending the fatherless and the oppressed,
in order that man, who is of the earth, may terrify no more.

"Sanctuary" – Woodcut from a Civil War sketch by Edwin Forbes

Thinking About It

•   This psalm brings doubt to the forefront. Why does God wait?

The psalmist is helpless before the wicked; he longs for God's rescue.

- Does this lament, prayed in desperation, resonate with you?

- Does the picture of the "wicked" ring true?

- What does the speaker want God to do about it all?

Psalms of Abolition

The Abolitionist movement in the U. S. was just getting up steam during the 1840's. Among Northern whites and free blacks, the driving force was the Congregational Church and the Society of Friends. These Christian groups took a positive stand in favor of abolition and publicly advocated a variety of anti-slavery initiatives.

As an integral part of their protest, the various abolitionist groups voiced their hope in terms of their common Christian faith. One manifestation of this was a song book, "Freedom's Lyre", copyright 1840, by Edwin Hatfield. This work, the author says in his preface,

> "….was undertaken at the request of the Executive Committee of the American Anti-Slavery Society. A work of this character has long been called for, by those who have been accustomed to meet and pray for the Emancipation of the Slave. No volume of a similar kind has heretofore been given to the American public. The materials, therefore, for such a work, are but few. In consequence, the compiler has admitted some hymns – more than he desired – which cannot be regarded as very poetical; but have been retained, because better, on the same subject, were not to be found."

> With the sincere hope that it may serve that it may serve to hasten the blessed day, when every yoke shall be broken, and every slave set free, it is now commended to The Friends of Freedom."

Many of the songs in "Freedom's Lyre" are framed as replies to or comments on specific psalms, like Psalm 10. "Song 5" is a sort of antiphon between this psalm of desperation and the abolitionist singer who also asks why God waits. Look for the flavor of the conversation – God's Word and the singer's verses in reply.

Song 5

"To avenge the oppressed." – Psalm 10

1 Why doth the Lord depart so far,
And why conceal his face,
When great calamaties appear,
And times of deep distress?

2 Lord, shall the wicked still deride,
Thy justice and thy laws?
Shall they advance their heads in pride,
And slight our righteous cause?

3 Arise O God! Lift up thine hand,
Attend our humble cry;
No enemy shall dare to stand,
When God, our help, is nigh.

4 Thou wilt prepare our hearts to pray,
And cause thine ear to hear;
Accept the vows thy children pay
And free thy saints from fear.

Watts

Dialog in Song and Verse

Psalm 10 anchors this hymn in an ongoing conversation with God. The heartsick abolitionist's conviction that he is doing God's work meshes with the plaintive complaint that God is waiting overlong to right this wrong of slavery.

This is an example of C. S. Lewis' point that, though we are all sinners, in the particular instance we pray about, we may well be in the right and anxious for God's judgment to come and straighten things out.

Notice that, like the psalms, the Song 5 doesn't ask for a particular punishment for evildoers, but rather asks that God make things right.

Psalm 103

Of David

1 Praise the Lord, O my soul;
all my innermost being, praise his Holy Name.

2 Praise the Lord, O my soul,
and forget not all his benefits –

3 who forgives all your sins
and heals all your diseases,

4 who redeems your life from the pit
and crowns you with love and compassion,

5 who satisfies your desires with good things
so that your youth is renewed like the eagle's.

6 The Lord works righteousness
and justice for all the oppressed.

7 He made known his ways to Moses,
his deeds to the people of Israel:

8 The Lord is compassionate and gracious,
slow to anger, abounding in love.

9 He will not always accuse,
nor will he harbor his anger forever;

10 he does not treat us as our sins deserve
or repay us according to our iniquities.

11 for as high as the heavens are above the earth,
so great is his love for those who fear him;

12 as far as the east is from the west,
so far has he removed our transgressions from us.

13 As a father has compassion on his children,
so the Lord has compassion on those who fear him;

14 For he knows how we are formed,
he remembers that we are dust.

15 As for man, his days are like grass,
he flourishes like a flower of the field;

16 the wind blows over it and it is gone,
and its place remembers it no more.

17 But from everlasting to everlasting
the Lord's love is with those who fear him,
and his righteousness with their children's children –

18 with those who keep his covenant
and remember to obey his precepts.

19 The Lord has established his throne in heaven
and his kingdom rules over all.

20 Praise the Lord, you his angels,
you mighty ones who do his bidding,
who obey his word.

21 Praise the Lord, all his heavenly hosts,
you his servants who do his will.

22 Praise the Lord all his works
everywhere in his dominion.

Praise the Lord O my soul.

Thinking About It

• Few people are blessed with a trouble-free life. Have you ever had to force yourself to pray? To worship?

• You rarely hear the old formula, "The Lord giveth and the Lord taketh away. Blest be the name of the Lord" any more. It is easy to forget that even the worst of the world's troubles aren't the last word. God, who did not spare his only Son on the cross, sees to that.

Luke Veldt was a Protestant mission developer in Spain when he lost his beloved thirteen-year old daughter Allison. Veld's book, "Written in Tears" is a heart wrenching though inspiring and honest description of the aftermath.

As he describes it,

> "You've heard people who have suffered a great loss compare the experience to a punch in the stomach or a kick in the head. You've heard it so often you don't hear it any more. It has lost its' impact. It's a cliché. Yet I can't describe our emotional state better than to say that each morning, one second after we awoke, we had the wind knocked out of us by the thought, "It wasn't a dream. Alli is gone." It is like a kick in the head. It knocks you off balance; it takes away your desire to move on.

> We didn't wish we were dead, but we didn't really care if we kept on living either." *(Veldt: 20)*

The Veldts, Luke and his wife Jodi, were left with five other children (one with Down's Syndrome) and a mission to care for. Luke's doubts and questions had to take second place to the stark necessity of his duties. He had to find a way to heal while pushing along through life.

Luke turned to the Bible for support, and eventually discovered Psalm 103, and its passage "As a father has compassion for his children, so the Lord has compassion for those who fear him, for he knows how we were made; he remembers that we are dust." (Psalm 103: 13-14).

The remainder of "Written in Tears" tells how he and Jodi used Psalm 103 as a lifeline to slowly reconnect them with God, their faith and to let them come to terms with Allison's death.

Luke Veldt's experience – letting God provide words his heart could not shape – is a help God offers to everyone who needs it. Luke's solace did not arrive through study, or throwing himself into his work, but through long, honest conversations with God, immersion in God's Word, and patient listening for God's answers.

Luther & family, 19th C. painting. Philip Melancthon is the guest..

Luther and Katie also lost beloved children.

Praying, even praying with the psalms, won't necessarily bring immediate relief. What prayer can do is allow you to feel God grieving with you, and allow you to regain a sense of balance that comes from knowing that your loved one is in God's loving hands. And so are you.

Psalm 15

A psalm of David.

1 Lord, who may dwell in your sanctuary?
Who may live on your holy hill?

2 He whose walk is blameless
 and who does what is righteous,
Who speaks the truth from his heart;

3 and has no slander on his tongue.

Who does his neighbor no wrong
and casts no slur on his fellowman,

4 Who despises a vile man
but honors those who fear the Lord,
who keeps his oath, even when it hurts.

5 who lends his money without usury
and does not accept a bribe against the innocent.

He who does these things will never be shaken.

Thinking About It

• What does God require of me?

Psalm 15 describes the life of the faithful one.

• Can I pray this? Can anyone meet this standard?

Maybe the specifics, but "walk blamelessly?" "Do what is righteous?" Are we only dealing with a statement of Law, intended to show us just how far we are from meeting God's standards?

• Is there gospel here?

If this is gospel and not law, it must refer to the kind of person God wants to make of us, not the kind we actually are, now.

Or else, something different is going on, here.

Interpreting the Hard Psalms

Dane Ortlund, Bible Publishing Director at Crossway, publisher of the English Standard Version (ESV) translation of the Bible, offers some help in his thought-provoking blog, "Strawberry-Rhubarb Theology". What follows is an explication of Dane's methodical extraction of the gospel inside this psalm. Following his pattern can lead you through many Bible difficulties. Here are the highlights.

Reading a difficult passage requires a step by step process. God's Word is in there, no matter what is blocking your understanding.

Don't worry about finding the Gospel too soon. That can lead to missing most of the message. The Gospel is in there, along with many other things God wants you to think about.

Listen to the psalm, hear what the psalmist is saying. Who is the psalmist talking to? In this case, someone who wants to be righteous, who is asking God (the Lord) how, and reporting back God's answer.

Look at the context. This is a psalm from Israel's public and private worship. It is addressed to the Lord, (YHWH) and it is asking for the Lord's own criteria.

Examine the question. Psalm 15 doesn't ask, "Who is good enough for God?", rather "who may dwell in your sanctuary?" and "Who may live on your holy hill?" "Holy Hill" refers to a particular place: Jerusalem – Mount Zion – the place where the "shekinah" or "glory" of God can be found. The underlying question is, "Who will be the recipient of the Lord's promises to Israel?" Who is God's promise intended for?

Look at the attributes of the one who receives God's blessings. The one who does what is righteous because he "walks blamelessly", who speaks, not just the truth, but "the truth from his heart". Who despises the vile but honors the upright. These are inner attitudes in line with visible behaviors. The one who may "dwell in the sanctuary" is, to use the old Cub Scout formula, morally "square". In ethical terms, this is someone who has integrity.

Notice also that the righteous one is fit to "dwell in" constant contact with God. One who can be in God's presence always. He is "blameless." In Old Testament language this does not mean one who is sinlessly perfect, but rather one who is completely loyal to YHWH.

This a standard to which we aspire when we dwell with God, rather than a set of entrance requirements we must meet before God will have anything to do with us. Again, integrity rather than perfection is the goal; perfection is the outcome after God takes over.

The upright person in Psalm 15 is the person God calls us to be. Can we get there? Can we "dwell in God's sanctuary"?

Let the Bible wrestle with the Bible. Remember Psalm 2, where God says, "I have installed my King on Zion, my holy hill." Christians identify this with Jesus, the Christ.

Jesus is the one, true inhabitant of God's Holy Hill. Jesus is the cornerstone of the Temple to be built on Zion – remember, in David's day the temple was unbuilt, but in the New Jerusalem, Jesus, the stone the builders rejected, is the cornerstone. We, his followers will be the temple, the place where God's spirit dwells.

Jesus the Son of God is ultimately the one who is fit to dwell in God's sanctuary, on Zion, God's Holy Hill. Dane observes, here, that in the last line of Psalm 15, "the one who does these things shall not be moved" is using the same verb and the same construction as Psalm 16, quoted by Peter in Acts 2:24-28 when he claims that because Jesus is at our right side, we also will not be shaken.

Psalms 15 and 16, supposedly devoid of Christian gospel, turn out to lead directly into a vow of trust in the risen Lord. The Hebrew Scriptures were written to lead us to Christ, and this "difficult" psalm does exactly that.

The complete article is available here [Downloaded 14 May 2013.]

http://en.wordpress.com/tag/strawberry-rhubarb-theology/

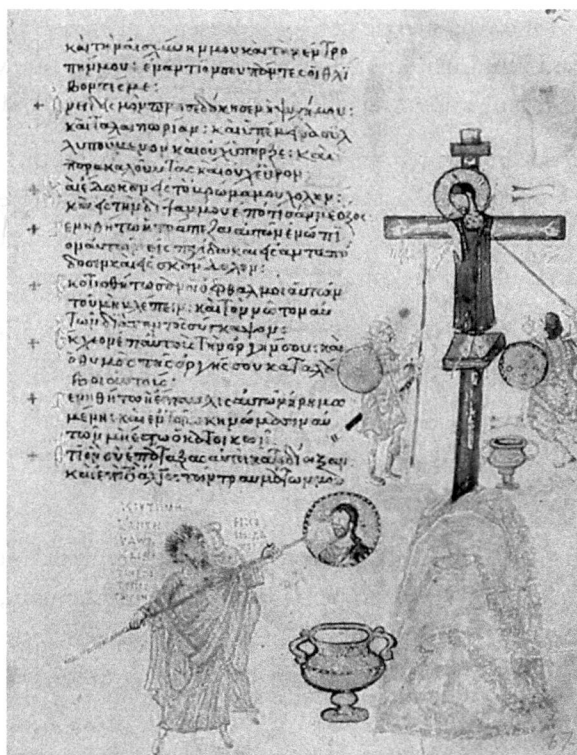

Chludov Psalter

Psalm 118

1 Give thanks to the Lord, for he is good;
his love endures forever.

2 Let Israel say:
"His love endures forever."

3 Let the House of Aaron say:
"His love endures forever."

4 Let those who fear the Lord say:
"His love endures forever."

5 In my anguish I cried to the Lord,
and he answered by setting me free.

6 The Lord is with me; I will not be afraid,
What can man do to me?

7 The Lord is with me, he is my helper.
I will look in triumph on my enemies.

8 It is better to take refuge in the Lord
than to trust in man.

9 It is better to take refuge in the Lord
than to trust in princes.

10 All the nations surrounded me,
but in the name of the Lord I cut them off.

11 They surrounded me on every side,
but in the name of the Lord I cut them off.

12 They swarmed around me like bees,
but they died out as quickly as burning thorns;
in the name of the Lord I cut them off.

13 I was pushed back and about to fall,
but the Lord helped me.

14 The Lord is my strength and my song;
he has become my salvation.

15 Shouts of joy and victory resound in the tents of the righteous;
the Lord's right hand has done mighty things!

16 The Lord's right hand is lifted high;
the Lord's right hand has done mighty things!

17 I will not die but live;
and will proclaim what the Lord has done.

18 The Lord has chastised me severely,
but he has not given me over to death.

19 Open for me the gates of righteousness;
I will enter and give thanks to the Lord.

20 This is the gate of the Lord
through which the righteous may enter.

21 I will give thanks, for you answered me;
you have become my salvation.

22 The stone the builders rejected
has become the capstone;

23 the Lord has done this,
and it is marvelous in our eyes.

24 This is the day the Lord has made,
let us rejoice and be glad in it.

25 O Lord, save us
O Lord, grant us success.

26 Blessed is he who comes in the name of the Lord.
From the house of the Lord we bless you.

27 The Lord is God,
and he has made his light shine upon us.

with boughs in hand, join in the festal procession
up to the horns of the altar.

28 You are my God and I will give you thanks;
you are my God and I will exalt you.

29 Give thanks to the Lord, for he is good;
his love endures forever.

Thinking About It

* This psalm compresses a number of themes expressed in the words from a familiar hymn, "God, our help in ages past, our hope in years to come".

* Sometimes giving extravagant thanks when God answers prayer is just what the moment calls for.

* From time to time it is good to "count our blessings", rejoice at what God has done and look forward to a wonderful future.

Book of Praises

For many the most difficult prayer is thanking God for blessings.

It is so much easier to see our troubles than to remember the good things God has already given us. Psalms is a reliable guide to praise. Praise which benefits us, rather than God. When we praise we don't overlook the abundant gifts he gives us or assume they are our due.

It is true that God's blessings are rich and creation is filled with them. God makes a brilliant sunrise every morning, whether we stop to enjoy it or not. Psalm 104, which we prayed in the first session, meditates on the breadth, depth and sheer abundance of God's gifts, the wonders he creates and sustains.

Thanksgivings in the Book of Psalms help to keep our focus on those abundant blessings, so we notice and enjoy them, and stop to give proper thanks to the God who distributes them lavishly.

Reflection – Summing up and Next Steps

The Psalter – Enchiridion of the Soul

Despite the name, Erasmus' Enchiridion was a theological argument disputing Luther's insistance that we are saved by Grace alone . The title implies it is something everyone should read.

An "Enchiridion" was a compact religious, philosophical or legal handbook. An old Greek word, the original enchiridion was a dagger a soldier carried in his pouch. If he were wounded and dying, the knife offered him a painless death. A Psalter, then, is an "Enchiridion" that prepares Christians for Heaven.

Your journey through the Psalms is the beginning of a pilgrimage that can last through the rest of your life – until you reach the Holy Hill and greet the One who invites us home.

Next Steps

Meantime, there are some concrete things you can do to build on the skills you gained from this exercise.

Adopt a Psalm reading program

Most hymnals have a schedule of suggested psalm readings adapted to the flow of the church year and its celebrations. An even simpler reading program is to begin at Psalm 1 and pray your way through, psalm by psalm, to Psalm 150. Take an extra day on the long psalms. Psalm 118 might last a week. This schedule will let you notice how the Psalms work slowly through the laments toward a vision of God's faithfulness in the final paean of thanksgiving of Psalm 150. It's a great way to experience the book as a whole and get the "big picture" God embedded in the Book of Psalms.

Find a Prayer partner

Meeting regularly with friends to read the Bible and pray together is one of the best ways to pray. You can also pool your prayer concerns for people you know, reminding you of God's concern for everyone without exception. Our Tuesday morning Bible study group sponsored by St. Timothy's Lutheran, San Jose CA is one of the most enjoyable benefits of belonging to my home congregation. Let some similar experience light up your life.

Selected reading

There are literally thousands of useful books about Psalms and hundreds that address using psalms in prayer. The following are accessible ways to learn more about the Psalms and topics discussed here. All were used in this study. They range across the modern spectrum of ecumenical Christian denominations, Reformed, Lutheran and Roman Catholic with an emphasis on the Lutheran tradition, which informs my own faith.

Bonhoeffer, Dietrich, "Psalms: The Prayerbook of the Bible".

Hatfield, Edward, "Freedom's Lyre" (S. W. Benedict, 1840) (Reprint 1969)

Mays, James Luther "The God Who Reigns", in Das, A. and Matera, F., editors, "The Forgotten God" (Westminster John Knox, 2002)

Lewis, C. S., "Reflections on the Psalms", (Harcourt Brace, 1958)

Limburg, James, "Psalms for Sojourners", James Burtness, translator, (Augsburg, 1986) Psalms as contemporary resources for prayer and praise.

Luther, Martin, "Psalms with Introductions", Bruce Cameron, translator (Concordia, 1993)

"How to Pray, for Peter the Barber"

http://www.ligonier.org/blog/martin-luther-prayer-free-download-sproul/

"Luther's Small Catechism with Explanation" (Concordia, 1991)

Murphy, Roland E. "Proclamation Commentaries: The Psalms, Job". (Fortress, 1982)

Thematic analysis by a noted Roman Catholic scholar.

Ortlund, Dane, "How do we read or preach a text like Psalm 15 in a Gospel way?" (posted 5 Dec 2012 on "Strawberry-Rhubarb Theology"

http://en.wordpress.com/tag/strawberry-rhubarb-theology/

Tiberius E. 1, "Of St. Theodora, virgin, who is also called Christina."

(MS in British Library @1139) This manuscript was certainly written by a monk who knew Christina personally and contains virtually all we know of her story. For a summary of current scholarship concerning Christina, Abbot Gregory and the St. Albans Psalter, see:

http://www.abdn.ac.uk/stalbanspsalter/english/index.shtml

Veldt, Luke, "Written in Tears, a Grieving Father's Journey through Psalm 103" (Discovery House, 2010). A missionary who lost his 13 year old daughter and his subsequent struggle with faith and trust.

Yancey, Philip, "The Bible Jesus Read" (Zondervan, 1999). Along with a good overview of the Christian content of the Old Testament, Yancey includes a relation of his personal encounter with praying the Psalms, with some consideration of their difficulties and lessons.

Commentaries

Two outstanding examples of the numerous short Bible commentaries useful for devotional reading:

Mays, James L., Harper-Collins Bible Commentary, Revised Ed. (HarperCollins, 2000).

Brown, Fitzmyer, Murphy "The New Jerome Biblical Commentary", (Prentiss Hall, 1999).

Quotations from the Scriptures

Psalms quoted in this study use the New International Version translation, except Psalm 23 and a quote from Isaiah, both of which are from the King James (Authorized) Version.

For readers who want a more literal translation, the Revised Standard Version, the English Standard Version, or the New Jerusalem Bible are very useful. The first two have English-Greek interlinear versions.

For personal devotions, Greek interlinear is not usually necessary. Scholars have extensively researched Koinoia Greek of Jesus' day and their work is reflected in the care taken to translate its meaning into modern languages.

Hebrew poetry maintains its essential meaning across language barriers, though its beauty varies according to the skill of the translator. Reading several different English translations will give you a feel for the rich imagery of the original, while the King James Version is itself exquisite Elizabethan English poetry.

Illustrations

Modern storytelling has become much easier since the advent of the internet. No longer must we search high and low for pertinent illustrations - they can be found and their copyright owners identified easily and quickly.

The illustrations used in this work are all in the public domain, or under a Creative Commons license.

Illustrations from medieval psalters show the range, the artistic merit and the importance of these manuscripts to Christians across a huge time span. Fortunately a number have survived.

Photographs of Dietrich Bonhoeffer are copyright by the Bundesarchiv, used with permission, or U.S. government photos, which are copyright free.

Acknowledgements and a personal note

Preparing this study has been a blessing and privilege. I was late coming to personal prayer as spiritual discipline. When I finally took the advice of older Christians, the change in my spiritual life has been wonderful.

I want to acknowledge my pastor who endured our Confirmation class so many years ago, Pastor Erwin Waltz, then of Holy Redeemer Lutheran Church, San Jose CA. His firm foundation and the Bible he taught me to love has been the rock I cling to in every sudden storm for over five decades now. Confirmation teachers are an extra-special ministry to the church and their young charges. They don't get enough credit.

I am also more than grateful to the St. Timothy's Lutheran Church, San Jose CA adult class, where a version of this study was initially presented. The comments, insights and response from this group assure me that God used our time together to deepen our faith, and their comments made this study much richer and more meaningful. Thank you all for participating.

And finally my wife Susan, who endured more than a year's research and preparation with more or less patience and forbearance: I couldn't have finished without you and your faith in the project. God bless.

Lawrence Duffield

June, 2013, San Jose CA

Visit my blog for comments and conversation:
cradlelutheran.wordpress.com